Author
Robin Jones

Production editor
Tim Hartley

Design
Justin Blackamore
Leanne Cropley
Charlotte Pearson
Tim Pipes

Front cover
Justin Blackamore

Marketing manager
Charlotte Park

Publisher
Steve O'Hara

Commercial director
Nigel Hole

Publishing director
Dan Savage

Published by
Mortons Media Group Ltd,
Media Centre, Morton Way,
Horncastle, Lincs LN9 6JR.
Tel: 01507 529529

Printed by
William Gibbons & Sons,
Wolverhampton
ISBN 978-1-911276-79-1

Note: pictures credited RM are reproduced courtesy of The Railway Magazine archives.

A HERITAGE RAILWAY PUBLICATION

© Mortons Media Group Ltd. All rights reserved. No part of this publication may be produced or transmitted in any form or by any means, electronic or mechanical, including photocopying, recording, or any information storage retrieval system without prior permission in writing from the publisher.

Introduction

A railway official with the withdrawal of services notice at Wellingborough London Road on 29 April 1964.
K FAIREY/COLOUR-RAIL.COM

Despite the fact that Britain invented the steam railway and introduced it to the rest of the world, surprisingly few of the names associated with this globe-shaping transport technology have become commonplace household words well outside the domains of the enthusiast and historian.

Among the elite group that have clearly managed this feat are *Flying Scotsman*, Stephenson's *Rocket* (no – despite the widespread popular misconception, George Stephenson did not invent the steam railway locomotive, that was down to Richard Trevithick), maybe *Royal Scot*, if only because of the marketing of the biscuit brand, perhaps *Mallard*, officially the world's fastest locomotive, and, dare I say it, Thomas the little blue engine. Another name that can be added to this list is that of Dr Richard Beeching.

Former British Railways chairman Dr Beeching has long been popularly portrayed as an axe-wielding ogre who closed as many railways as he could, got rid of the universally-loved steam engines and left communities all over Britain with no access to trains.

Indeed, a mistake often made in print is referring to a particular branch line as a 'Beeching closure' when he had nothing at all to do with it, the particular withdrawal of services taking place before his appointment to the British Railway Board in 1961.

Many people still hold the view that if the dreaded doctor had not descended on the nation's railways in the Sixties, many of the closed lines would still be running today. Some of the more informed among us have from the start seriously questioned the criteria used by him and those that came afterwards to justify the closure of individual routes, particularly those serving large centres of population.

Mountains of hindsight are regularly expressed with the aim of expressing the view that Beeching was wrong in this or that case, that route closures were premature, and if only the powers that be had foreseen the expansion of rural communities in commuter belt country, and the nightmarish road congestion from the 1980s onwards, in which households on even very modest incomes support two or maybe three second-hand cars, the decisions regarding the wholesale pruning of the rail network in the Sixties may have been very different.

In several, though by no means all, of these 'lost line' scenarios, it is difficult not to sympathise or agree wholeheartedly, but it is so easy to pass judgment long after the event, without looking at the circumstances that prevailed at the time when many hard decisions were made.

Coming into the sector from a purely business point of view, in 1963 he produced a report, *The Reshaping of British Railways*, which became one of the seminal documents of British railway history.

It led to the closure of around a third of the nation's railway network, throwing tens of thousands of railwaymen on to the dole queue, disenfranchising some of the country's biggest towns from train services as well as country branches lines, in a vain bid to cut the soaring British Railways deficit in an age where passenger numbers dwindled as car ownership ran rampant. On the other hand, it also streamlined the network in a way that helped ensure its survival into the 21st century, an era in which passenger numbers are now at their highest for many decades.

So was Beeching a villain – or a hero? The story of the man who probably had the biggest impact on the nation's railways since George and Robert Stephenson invented *Rocket* is outlined in this special publication more than five decades after his controversial appointment.

Robin Jones

Nearly two decades after it was closed under the Beeching Axe and its tracks ripped up, lonely Penygroes station on the Caerrnarfon to Afon Wen line stands as a stark reminder of the brutal rail closures of the sixties. MIKE ESAU

The ring of doom – a closure proposal notice being read by a member of staff working the intermediate stations on the electrified Woodhead line in 1964. Although these intermediate halts would go, and local freight would also be withdrawn, Beeching saw this Manchester-Sheffield line as a shining example of the future of British Rail! Unfortunately, express traffic also failed to survive the decade on this useful cross-country link, which had made national headlines because of its modernisation in 1954.
ALAN EARNSHAW COLLECTION

The Dalmellington branch of the former Glasgow & South Western Railway was one of the Ayrshire lines to lose its passenger services from April 6, 1964. BR Standard 3M T 2-6-0 No 77016 heads the last steam train – and the penultimate service – over the branch two days earlier. DEREK CROSS/RM

Contents

CHAPTER 1:
The road back to roads

CHAPTER 2:
The Marples master plan

CHAPTER 3:
Cometh the hour, cometh the axeman

CHAPTER 4:
The times they are a-changing

CHAPTER 5:
The Reshaping of British Railways

CHAPTER 6:
The rationale and the results

CHAPTER 7:
The backlash and backpedalling

CHAPTER 8:
The whole world turns blue

CHAPTER 9:
Beeching Mark 2

CHAPTER 10:
More closures, followed by compassion

CHAPTER 11:
The end of mass closures

CHAPTER 12:
Great Beeching survivors

CHAPTER 13:
Reopenings as heritage railways

CHAPTER 14:
The unravelling of the cuts

CHAPTER 15:
The final verdict

Left: The Amlwch branch in Anglesey closed on December 7, 1964. Ivatt 2-6-2 tank engine No 41226 is seen at Amlwch with the 1.08pm service from Gaerwen on August 26, that year. ANDREW MUCKLEY/RM

Right: *The Reshaping of British Railways*, Dr Richard Beeching's report of 1963 which changed the face of transport in the UK.

Chapter One

The road *back to roads*

Right: **Richard Trevithick built self-propelled road vehicles before he turned to railway locomotives.**

Below: **In 1802, Trevithick demonstrated his pioneer London Steam Carriage in the capital, offering trips from the city centre to Paddington and back, with up to eight guests on board. It lays claim to being the world's first motor bus, and the first official public run of a self-powered passenger vehicle. This modern-day replica built by Tom Brogden is seen in Regent's Park in 2003.**

The essence of the postwar controversy about rail closures has its roots long before Dr Richard Beeching, and might be considered to date back to the birth of the steam locomotive itself.

Cornish mining engineer Richard Trevithick, frustrated at his home county's isolation from the canal network which provided the trade arteries of the Industrial Revolution, and indeed the poor communications between Cornwall and the rest of Britain apart from by sea, followed up earlier rudimentary experiments with horseless carriages by building his own steam locomotive – but one which would run on roads. Trevithick and engineer Andrew Vivian built a steam road carriage which, on Christmas Eve 1801, climbed Camborne Hill under its own power. Onlookers jumped aboard for a ride – and so was born the world's first motor car!

The obvious advantage of road transport over rail is its great versatility. It does not rely on the provision of railway tracks and offers almost infinite personal choice and freedom for travel.

However, back in the early 19th century, the great Roman art of roadbuilding had largely been forgotten and in those days before the invention of Tarmacadam, most of them were muddy potholed affairs which even horses and carts found uncomfortable.

In 1802, Trevithick demonstrated his pioneer London Steam Carriage in the capital, offering trips from the city centre to Paddington and back, with up to eight guests on board. It was the world's first motor bus, and the first official public run of a self-powered passenger vehicle.

However, steering was the big problem and the carriage ended up crashing into railings. The fault lay not with the vehicle, but with the poor bumpy roads.

Trevithick built a second carriage for London in 1803. Standing 13ft high, it proved too big and could not compete economically with the horse-drawn versions.

He finally overcame the problem of inadequate roads by using rails on which to run his steam locomotives. In 1802, he built a steam railway locomotive for private use at Coalbrookdale ironworks in Shropshire, and two years later gave the world's first public demonstration of one on the Penydarren Tramroad near Merthyr Tydfil.

Above: **On February 21, 1804, Trevithick gave the world's first public demonstration of a railway locomotive, hauling 10 tons of iron over the horse-drawn tramroad linking Penydarren ironworks near Merthyr Tydfil to the Glamorganshire Canal. A replica built in Wales in 1981 from Trevithick's original documents and plans is seen in action at the National Railway Museum.** ROBIN JONES

Right: **Richard Trevithick and engineer Andrew Vivian constructed a steam road carriage which ascended Camborne Hill in Cornwall under its own power on Christmas Eve 1801. Delighted watchers jumped aboard, making it the world's first motor car – and it emerged at least a year before the first self-propelled railway locomotive! The Trevithick Society's replica is pictured at the Railfest 200 event in 2004 at the National Railway Museum in York.** ROBIN JONES

Had the roads of the day been capable of carrying his road steam locomotives, would there have been any point in him looking at rail?

Nevertheless, the world at large was slow on the uptake of Trevithick's locomotives. The shortage of horses caused by the army needing so many for the Napoleonic Wars led to mine owners in the north of England looking for alternative traction for their private tramways in the early part of the decade that followed; but it was not until 1825 that the world's first public steam-operated railway, the Stockton & Darlington, opened, and even then locomotives were at first used for freight, with horses pulling passenger trains.

It was *Rocket's* triumph in the Rainhill Trials of 1829 and the Liverpool & Manchester Railway's adoption of steam locomotive traction that finally steered the railway concept on the course to transport supremacy and opened the floodgates for the years of railway mania, in which a multitude of speculative schemes sought to connect city with city, town with town, and in carving up the British mainland, created the basis of the national network for the centuries that followed.

The railways linked industrial centres to ports, facilitated the development of dormitory towns and commuter belts, took farming produce to national markets and opened up the seaside to mass tourism, among many other benefits too many to mention here. They made it easier for country folk to migrate to the expanding cities in search of a better life. In Victorian times, the railway not only reshaped society but became a backbone of it.

Beeching: 55 Years of the Axe Man **7**

Expanded to its limits

The Kent & East Sussex Railway may be regarded as the epitome of the cut-price rural lines built under the 1896 Light Railways Act, with basic infrastructure and low construction costs. The Act began the last swathe of railway building before the emergence of motor transport. A special from London Victoria via the main line connection at Robertsbridge is seen arriving at Tenterden, heading by LBSCR 'Terrier' tank No 32670, with sister DS680 Waddon on the rear.
HUGH BALLANTYNE

By and large, the railway network had expanded to its maximum size by the dawn of the 20th century. Towards the end of Victorian times, efforts were made to connect the remaining parts of the country not deemed profitable enough to warrant attention from the major railway operators to the national network.

The Light Railways Act 1896 was a response to the economic downturn of the previous decade that had hit agriculture and rural communities hard. It made it far easier to build a rural railway 'on the cheap' without having to apply for a costly Act of Parliament. The act limited weights to a maximum of 12 tons on each axle and line speeds to a maximum of 25mph. Such limitations allowed the use of lightly laid track and relatively modest bridges in order to keep costs down. Also, level crossings did not have to have gates, just cattle grids.

The act led to nearly 30 local standard and narrow gauge railways being built under its powers, the best-known examples perhaps being the Kent & Sussex Light Railway, which opened in 1900, the Basingstoke and Alton Light Railway of 1901, the Vale of Rheidol Railway in 1902, the Welshpool & Llanfair Light Railway in 1903 and the Leek & Manifold Valley Light Railway and the Tanat Valley Light Railway of 1904.

By contrast, in 1899, under railway magnate Edward Watkin, the Manchester, Sheffield & Lincolnshire Railway opened its 'London Extension' from Annesley, north of Nottingham, to Marylebone and changed its name to the Great Central Railway.

It was the last trunk railway to be built in Britain until the Channel Tunnel Rail Link from St Pancras International a century later; indeed, it was Watkin's intention for it to link up with a proposed Channel Tunnel, and accordingly it was built to continental loading clearances to allow potential through running of trains to and from Europe.

Also in 1899, the Great Western Railway obtained an Act of Parliament permitting construction of a double-track railway between Honeybourne and Cheltenham and doubling of the single-track route from Stratford-upon-Avon to Honeybourne. This would link in with the North Warwickshire Line being built from Tyseley to Stratford via Bearley Juntion to provide a through route from the Midlands to the south west to compete with the Midland Railway route via the Lickey Incline.

Work began on construction of the Honeybourne-Cheltenham line in November in 1902, and it was opened throughout four years later.

In 1910, the first through trains over the route between Wolverhampton, Birmingham and the West Country and Cardiff were introduced. It may be considered as the last great cross-country route to be completed.

Railway building did not end there, but new lines that were subsequently opened were very much local affairs, such as the North Devon & Cornwall Junction Light Railway, which made use of existing mineral lines to link Halwill Junction to Torrington from July 27, 1925.

However, history recorded that, in short, virtually everywhere that was going to be connected to the rail network had been reached by Edwardian times.

The big threat emerges

The improvements in roads made in Britain following the development of the 'Macadam' type of surface pioneered by Scotsman John Loudon McAdam around 1820 led to renewed interest by inventors in looking at self-propelled forms of transport that could run over them.

The International Exposition of Electricity in Paris held in November 1881 saw French inventor Gustave Trouvé demonstrate a working three-wheeled automobile powered by electricity.

German engineer Karl Benz is generally hailed as the inventor of the modern car.

He constructed a three-wheeled carriage-like road vehicle powered by his own four-stroke cycle gasoline engine in Mannheim in 1885, and the following year his company, Benz & Cie, was granted a patent. The company began to sell automobiles off its production line in 1888, and sold around 25 of them between then and 1893, when his first four-wheeler appeared.

In 1896, Benz designed and patented the first internal-combustion flat engine, and by the end of the century, was the world's largest automobile company.

The first design for an American automobile with a gasoline internal combustion engine was produced by George Selden of New York in 1877.

In Britain, Thomas Rickett tried a production run of steam cars in 1860. Charles Santler of Malvern is regarded as having built the first petrol-powered car in the country in 1894, but it was a one-off. The first production automobiles in Britain came from the Daimler Motor Company in 1897.

Industrial-scale car production began in the USA in 1902, at the Oldsmobile plant in Lansing,

A 1910 Model T Ford pictured in Salt Lake City, Utah, the following year. The challenge to railway's supremacy had begun! HARRY SHIPLER

Henry Ford pictured in 1919.

Michigan. Henry Ford's Model T came on the scene in 1908, and soon his Detroit factory was turning out cars at 15-minute intervals. Not only that, but he had also made the car affordable: by 1914, when 250,000 Model Ts had been sold, an assembly line worker could buy a Model T with four months' pay.

Ford Britain was founded in 1911 and in 1921, Citroen became the first European car manufacturer to adopt Ford's ground-breaking production line methods. By 1930, all manufacturers had followed suit, and while it was at first much regarded as a rich man's plaything, with railway travel the primary option for much of the population, car ownership was very much in the ascendancy.

Ivatt 2-6-2 tank engine No 41295 pauses at Petrockstowe with the single-coach 8.52am service from Torrington to Halwill Junction on 4 July 1956. This particular line was not built until 1925, well into the motor transport era. HUGH BALLANTYNE

Competing against itself

A railway company does not necessarily imply that it exists to promote the railway concept; the key word is 'company', a body that is created to generate profits by the best means possible.

When the dawn of the 20th century saw that motor road vehicles would shape the future of transport later if not sooner, the Great Western Railway looked at providing bus services not only as a feeder to its train services, but also as a cheaper alternative to building new branch lines in sparsely populated rural areas which would never pay. The GWR baulked at the idea of spending £85,000 on extending the Helston branch with a light railway to Britain's southernmost village, Lizard Town, and decided to try motor buses instead.

Two vehicles that had been used temporarily by the Lynton & Barnstaple Railway were acquired, the service was launched on August 17, 1903, the summer before City class 4-4-0 No 3440 *City of Truro* unofficially became the first steam locomotive in the world to break the 100mph barrier, with a speed of 102.3mph recorded hauling the 'Ocean Mails Special' from Plymouth to Paddington on May 9, 1904.

The idea of a railway company running a motor bus dated back to 1890, when the Belfast & Northern Counties Railway fitted seats to a petrol-engined parcels delivery van and took fares for rides in it.

The Lizard buses proved so popular and profitable other routes were soon established, first locally to Mullion, Ruan Minor and Porthleven, and then further afield at Penzance.

A bus route from Slough station to Beaconsfield was launched on March 1, 1904, followed by routes to Windsor on July 18 that year. Indeed, the first GWR double deckers appeared on the Slough-Windsor service in 1904 onwards.

A route from Wolverhampton to Bridgnorth was briefly operated from November 7, 1904 using steam buses, motor buses replacing them the following year.

By the end of 1904, 36 buses were in GWR operation, and the Great Western Railway (Road Transport) Act was passed in 1928; the GWR boasted the biggest railway bus fleet. This act paved the way for the services to be transferred to bus companies, although the railway was to be a shareholder in these operations. On January 1, 1929, the GWR routes in Devon and Cornwall went over to the new Western National Omnibus Company, 50% owned by the railway and the other half by the National Omnibus

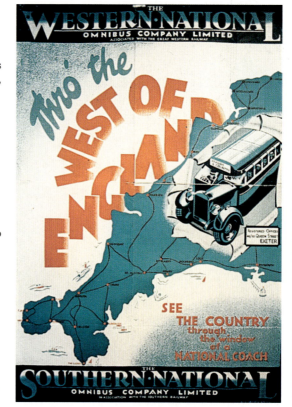

Poster advertising the start of GWR bus services from Helston to Lizard Town on 17 August 1903, an experiment which began as an alternative to building a railway line and rapidly evolved into a competitor to rail services.

and Transport Company. That year the GWR acquired 30 per cent of the shares in the Devon General Omnibus and Touring Company.

The final bus services operated by the GWR began in the Weymouth area in 1935, jointly run with the London & South Western Railway, and were transferred to Southern National on 1 January, 1934.

Never afraid to compete with the railway concept, on April 11, 1933, the GWR launched its first air service, flying from Cardiff to Exeter and Plymouth.

The GWR and the other major railway operators built up extensive fleets of lorries and vans to supplement rail freight services. Yet what would happen when the day came that road vehicles would no longer supplement goods trains, but carry freight from start to finish in their own right?

Great Western Railway motor bus No 1278.

Above: **While rail technology reached the point where steam locomotives broke the 100mph barrier, as was said to have happened with GWR 4-4-0 No 3440 *City of Truro* in 1904, buses were emerging as a potential competitior. *City of Truro*, now owned by the National Railway Museum and restored in time for the centenary of the unofficial record-breaking run, is seen at Horse Cove between Dawlish and Teignmouth with Pathfinder Tours' 'Ocean Mail 100' from Kingswear to Bristol in May 2004.** BRIAN SHARPE

Road freight on the rise

Britain would never be the same after the First World War. One of the marked changes was the blurring of the distinction between social classes: public schoolboys and labourers alike had experienced the horrors of the Western Front together, and never again would it be a case of one doffing their cap to the other. Similarly, churchgoing rapidly declined after 1918, with religion becoming less relevant to a population bemused at why it had not been able to prevent the carnage of the trenches.

There was a fresh spirit of entrepreneurship among the soldiers returning from the front. Large quantities of road vehicles became sold off as military surplus, and many were eagerly bought up by those wishing to launch their own haulage businesses. In doing so, freight was switched slowly but surely from rail to the cheaper and more versatile road alternative.

In turn, local authorities began to build more roads to cater for the increase in traffic.

Because of the growth of road haulage, the railways' profit margins began to suffer. The road hauliers could offer significantly lower prices than the railways, while offering the benefits of door-to-door delivery, while the railways were hampered by their original charters of the 1840s and 50s to act as common carriers, and legally were unable to refuse unprofitable cargoes and lower their transportation costs accordingly.

A series of Royal Commissions into the problem was held in the 30s, but failed to find a solution. Chancellor of the Exchequer Neville Chamberlain, who as prime minister is best known for his 'peace in our time' appeasement of Hitler, increased vehicle excise duty, leaving the hauliers

The surviving buildings of Whitwick station on the Charnwood Forest Railway, an early standard gauge closure.
MALTAGC/CREATIVE COMMONS

Manning Wardle 2-6-2T Taw in Southern Railway livery heads a Lynton & Barnstaple Railway passenger train into Woody Bay station only a few days before the line closed in 1935. Several other light railways went under around this time, due to competition from road transport, while other countries similarly experienced swathes of early branch line closures. R L KNIGHT

paying all of the Annual Road Fund. This was a big boost to the railways, who were now theoretically back in the driving seat, but before they could reap big dividends from it, the Second World War broke out. Furthermore, the railways were not released from their historic common carrier obligations until 1957.

Dr Beeching did not invent main line railway closures: that was a process that may be deemed to have begun more than a century before he came on the transport scene. In 1851, the Newmarket & Chesterford Railway closed its Great Chesterford to Six Mile Bottom section after opening a more viable length linking Six Mile Bottom straight to Cambridge.

The First World War saw a comparatively small number of rural railways closed, with their tracks lifted for use on the Western Front military lines, never to reopen again. These included the Bideford, Westward Ho! & Appledore Railway, and the GWR line from Rowington to Henley-in-Arden, which had been superseded by the North Warwickshire Line, but were still small beer in the overall scheme of railways.

The 1930s, however, saw a swathe of closures of many 'rural fringe' lines, the like of which had been empowered by the 1896 Light Railways Act. Some, like the GWR-run Welshpool & Llanfair and Corris railways, lost their passenger services but remained open for freight, while others, like the Lynton & Barnstaple, by then part of the Southern Railway, the Welsh Highland Railway and the Leek & Manifold Valley Railways, closed outright.

The standard gauge Charnwood Forest Railway in Leicestershire ceased running passenger trains in 1931, and Birmingham's Harborne branch closed to passengers in 1934 in the face of direct competition from trams and motor buses.

The Weston, Clevedon & Portishead Railway, the only direct route of any description between those three towns, ran its last public train in 1940.

Few of these can be regarded as mainstays of the railway network; indeed, regardless of their historical or romantic appeal, it is debatable whether some of them should have been built at all, and once the motor road vehicle provided a creditable alternative, it is all but certain that they would not have been. In any event, so many of the 1896 Act railways had a lifespan of only around three decades, and their demise gave a strong pointer to the future of rural lines.

Many view the 1930s as the zenith of Britain's railway network. This poster advertises the classic 'Coronation Scot', a named luxury streamlined express passenger train of the London, Midland & Scottish Railway, inaugurated in 1937 for the coronation of King George VI and which ran between Euston and Glasgow Central, and was headed by chief mechanical engineer William Stanier's Princess Coronation Pacific locomotives. On the London & North Eastern Railway's rival route to Scotland, Nigel Gresley's A4 Pacific No. 4468 *Mallard* set the world rail speed record on July 3, 1938 when it hit 125.88mph on Stoke Bank on the East Coast Main Line in Lincolnshire. NRM

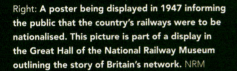

Right: **A poster being displayed in 1947 informing the public that the country's railways were to be nationalised. This picture is part of a display in the Great Hall of the National Railway Museum outlining the story of Britain's network.** NRM

Nationalisation: the 'Big Four' become one

The big watershed in the history of Britain's railways in 1948 came when the national network was taken into permanent public ownership for the first time.

The nation's railways had been placed under state control during the First World War, and it was clear that the network could be run more efficiently with fewer operators. Afterwards there were calls for complete nationalisation – a move first mooted in 1850. However, the Railways Act 1921 provided a compromise with the grouping of most of the country's 120 railway companies into four main ones. These were the 'Big Four' – comprising the Great Western Railway, the London, Midland & Scottish Railway, the London & North Eastern Railway and the Southern Railway.

The Second World War again saw the nation's railways acting as one company, a time when the network saw more use than at any other point in its history.

Luftwaffe air raids inflicted heavy damage, particularly around London and Coventry, while the diversion of resources from maintenance led to the network falling into disrepair. After the war, it was soon realised that the private sector could not afford to put right the damage and decay, and so Clement Attlee's Labour government decided to nationalise the railways under the Transport Act 1947. British Railways came into existence as the business name of the Railway Executive of the British Transport Commission.

It was clear from the start that there would be closures. The Railway Executive was fully aware that some lines on the very dense network were unprofitable and also difficult to justify on social grounds. Going back to the Victorian era of Railway Mania, it is easy to argue that too many lines, particularly local branches, were built that history was to show could never really be justified. In terms of long-distance travel, there soon arose competition between different companies for the same passengers. One famous example was the 'Races to the North' whereby rivals competed to see who could take passengers from London to Scotland fastest, while the GWR and London & South Western Railway, later Southern Railway, competed strongly for the London-Exeter-Plymouth markets, as did the GWR and LMS for London-Birmingham, to quote another of many examples. While such rival routes served different communities along the way, if inter-city travel was considered of paramount important, then a logical step forward would be to pick the best route and divert all the resources to that, and maybe consider the other for closure.

The first official closure under British Railways was the goods-only line from Mantle Lane East to the foot of Swannington Incline in Leicestershire, by the new London Midland Region, in February 1948. The first passenger services to be withdrawn were those from Woodford & Hinton station on the Great Central route, to Byfield on the Stratford & Midland Junction Railway, on May 31, 1948, also by the LMR.

Another of the very early closures was that of the 2ft 3in gauge Corris Railway, inherited from the GWR, which was axed following flood damage on August 21, 1948.

The following year, the British Transport Commission set up the Branch Lines Committee, with a remit to close the least-used branch lines.

The modest programme of closures continued in 1949 with passenger services withdrawn from Liverpool Lime Street to Alexandra Dock, Stratford-upon-Avon to Broom, and Fenchurch Street to Stratford (Bow Junction). In 1950, a total of 150 route miles were closed, rising to 275 in 1951 and 300 in 1952.

The Northern Eastern railway branch line north of Tow Law to Blackhill in County Durham lost its passenger service as early as May 1939. The line south from Tow Law to Crook closed on June 11, 1956. LNER A5 4-6-2T No. 69836 is seen with a passenger train at Tow Law in the early 1950s. BEAMISH MUSEUM

Still steaming on

Above: The first of 999 British Railways standard locomotives: Pacific No. 70000 *Britannia*, in black livery rather than its familiar Brunswick green and minus nameplates, undergoes test running on the West Coast Main Line north of Crewe prior to its official naming by Transport Minister Alfred Barnes at Marylebone on January 30, 1951. British Railways would still be building steam engines for several years after deciding to switch over to diesel and electric traction.
COLOUR-RAIL.COM 19062

By the late 1940s, Britain was lagging behind other major countries in terms of the phasing out of steam traction.

The LMS produced its first diesel shunter in 1931, and in December 1947, the month before Nationalisation, unveiled Britain's first main line diesel locomotive to the waiting press.

Derby-built Co-Co No. 10000 had made its first run the month before, and after proving trials entered service in February 1948, followed by sister No. 10001. They became British Railway's D16/1 class. In 1950-51, the Southern Region's Ashford Works turned out two prototype main line diesel locomotives, which became Class D16/2.

In 1934, the Great Western Railway introduced the first of a very successful series of railcars, which were used on cross-country services and which survived in regular use into the 1960s. The GWR also ordered two gas turbine locomotives.

However, these developments were a drop in the ocean compared with the modernisation taking place in the United States and elsewhere.

While steam locomotives are labour intensive regarding maintenance and operation, diesels need much less time and labour to operate and maintain. A fire has to be built in a steam locomotive firebox several hours before it runs: a diesel is not dissimilar from a car, which just needs the turning of an ignition key. Also, while electrification of railway lines by providing overhead masts has a high capital outlay, the operating costs are much lower.

Following legislation of 1923 banning the use of steam locomotives within New York City, railroads turned to diesels, the Central Railroad of New Jersey introducing its first in 1925. By the Thirties, dieselisation was well underway, and most trunk railroads had retired all of their steam locomotives by the mid 1950s, although some, albeit in ever-diminishing numbers, continued on short lines into the Sixties, with a rare stragglers lasting in revenue-earning service until the Seventies. For the record, the Crab Orchard & Egyptian Railroad, a steam-using tourist line which added regular revenue freight service in 1977, is said to be the last US railroad of any kind to use steam locomotives in regular service, as opposed to operation for tourist or heritage purposes.

Canadian Pacific ordered its first diesel in 1937, turned out its last new steam locomotive in 1949 and completed dieselisation by 1960.

Much closer to home, the Irish Republic introduced main line diesel railcars in 1950, the same year that its railways were nationalised into Córas Iompair Éireann, a move which led to widespread closures of loss-making lines. In 1955, it made large scale diesel purchases within five years, virtually all steam on scheduled main line passenger services was over. CIE eliminated steam altogether in 1962.

In the early years of nationalisation, Britain was still emerging from the effects of the war and years of austerity. British Railways had inherited a locomotive fleet which included numerous ancient types that had long since been overtaken by technology, and needed new engines and fast

Dieselisation, a move which was clearly inevitable, was seen by the powers-that-be as taking a leap in the dark at that time, and so when Robert Riddles, the Ministry of Supply's director of transportation equipment during the

Right: Austin cars new off the production line in 1948, ready to fulfil the demands of a rapidly-growing car-owning society.

14 *Beeching: 55 Years of the Axe Man*

Above: The 1950s were not the first time that 'modern' traction in the form of railcars was introduced in a bid to make branch line travel more attractive. The trials of a steam railmotor – a carriage with a steam engine built into a compartment at one end and which can also be controlled from another – on the Great Western railway's Golden Valley line at Stroud in 1903 were so successful in boosting passenger numbers that 99 were built.

They had the advantage of being able to operate from small cheap platforms and halts and also to compete on suburban lines against the new electric tramways.

However, railmotors proved difficult to maintain and at busy times, such as market days, they could not cope with passenger demand.

On March 21, 2011, the Didcot-based Great Western Society unveiled its restored steam railmotor No 93, dating from 1908 and now the only one of its type in the world, and the culmination of a 15-year project.

It is seen at Glyndyfrdwy station on the Llangollen Railway alongside that line's award-winning restored Class 109 Wickham two-car diesel multiple unit No 56171, which was built in 1958 as one of the many first-generation British Railways types intended to save rural branches and country tourers. While such DMUs were welcomed by the public in the Fifties, their introduction was not enough to prevent many branch lines closure before Beeching's appointment. ROBIN JONES

Right: The spacious modern art deco interior of the 1958 Wickham diesel multiple unit offered new luxury and comfort on country branch and suburban trains, but was it too little, too late? ROBIN JONES

Beeching: 55 Years of the Axe Man **15**

Second World War and a former vice-president of the LMS, was appointed Member of the Railway Executive for Mechanical and Electrical Engineering in 1948, effectively the old post of chief mechanical engineer, he stuck with steam.

British Railways continued to build locomotives to old 'Big Four' designs, and turned out a total of 2537.

Riddles, meanwhile, oversaw the development of new 'Standard' designs, of which 999 were built. The Standards drew largely from LMS designs, but incorporated some features from the other Big Four companies' locomotives.

The first Standard was Pacific No. 70000 *Britannia*, which emerged from Crewe Works in 1951, the year of the Festival of Britain.

Many believe that the BR Standard 9F 2-10-0s were the best of the Riddles designs. They were built to last 40 years. The final Standard design was a one-off, 8P Pacific No. 71000 *Duke of Gloucester*, built in 1954.

Despite the excellence of many Standard designs, history records that they were just a stop gap, with their days numbered as the UK economy began to recover.

That is not to say that steam was not capable of holding its win. By the late Fifties maintenance had slowly but surely been brought back up to date, and long-distance schedules were generally back on par with those of the 1930s.

Measures were taken to enhance the performance of prewar locomotives working in postwar conditions: for example, the Western Region equipped all the King 4-6-0s and many Castle 4-6-0s with double chimneys to improve their steaming; Bulleid's streamlined Pacifics were rebuilt without their distinctive air-smooth casings and all of the Gresley Pacifics had been fitted with Kylchap blastpipes and double chimneys, a move especially effective with the A3s.

Vintage lorries on display at Crewe Works. The availability of military surplus road vehicles after the First World War led to competition which would eventually kill off many local rail freight services. ROBIN JONES

However, in 1954, the Leeds/Bradford area of the West Riding of Yorkshire was chosen by British Railways as a pilot area in which to test the first of its diesel multiple units, a type of vehicle following on from the GWR diesel railcars, and previous LMS experimental vehicles. Also, in June that year, the electrified Woodhead route between Manchester and Sheffield, a project first proposed by the LNER, was completed, with the electric services inaugurated that September.

Another big factor at this time which was carving into the railways' viability was the denationalisation of road transport. The road haulage industry had bitterly opposed nationalisation by the Attlee government. After the Conservatives were elected in 1951, road haulage was soon denationalised and deregulated. Again, it could offer charges which greatly undercut those of rail, while the still-heavily regulated railways, which had to meet the extra burden of safety costs, remained under the control of the British Transport Commission.

Below: **Not the way ahead: in the late 1940s the Great Western Railway ordered two experimental gas turbine locomotives for express passenger work, one from Metropolitan Vickers of Manchester, the other from the Swiss manufacturer Brown Boveri. They were delivered in 1949 after Nationalisation and entered regular service. While their performance showed promise, the gas turbine principle was not ultimately adopted and this pair effectively ended in a cul-de-sac. Metropolitan Vickers No. 18100 is seen with 'The Merchant Venturer' at Bristol Temple Meads station on May 31, 1952.** T E WILLIAMS/NRM

The British Railways Modernisation Plan

As the financial situation eased, the inevitable happened on December 1, 1954: British Railways unveiled its blueprint for the future.

The report known as Modernisation and Re-Equipment of the British Railways, or the 1955 Modernisation Plan for short, despite the fact it was published at the end of the previous year, set out to combat the threat presented to the railways by road transport.

The target was to increase speed, reliability, safety and line capacity, while making services more attractive to passengers and freight operators.

The most notable aim was the complete phasing out of steam locomotives by diesel and electric alternatives. It also proposed the electrification of principal main lines, including the East Coast Main Line to Leeds and possibly York, the Great Northern suburban system, Euston to Birmingham/Manchester/ Liverpool, Chelmsford to Clacton/Ipswich/Felixstowe; the Liverpool Street north-east suburban system; Fenchurch Street to Tilbury and Shoeburyness; and the Glasgow north suburban network.

Initial proposals to employ the overhead I500V of the Woodhead route were discarded once the advantages of the 25kV AC were fully realised. South of the Thames, in long-established third-rail electric territory, it was intended to electrify all main lines east of Reading-Portsmouth. Elsewhere, diesels would replace steam.

The report also proposed a new fleet of passenger and freight rolling stock, the creation of large goods marshalling yards with automated shunting to streamline freight handling, mass resignalling and track renewal, and the closure of more unprofitable lines and routes which duplicated others. The report proposed to spend £1240 million over 15 years to achieve these goals.

In 1956, a government White Paper confidently stated that modernisation would help eliminate BR's financial deficit by 1962.

However, at a time when British Railways was still turning out large numbers of steam locomotives, the observer might be forgiven for getting the impression that the left hand did not know what the right hand was doing. History records that this indeed turned out to be the case, and the deficit would certainly not disappear.

The Railway Executive's initial plan to keep steam on busy routes until it was superseded by electric traction was abandoned, and instead, diesels would provide a stop-gap until electrification, while on secondary lines, they would provide the long-term solution.

Steam continued to be built for the national network until March 25, 1960, when Swindon Works ceremoniously outshopped the last Standard 9F, No. 92220 *Evening Star*, while at the same time, British Railways rushed headlong into ordering a motley assortment of main line diesel types which were to show that they might have been far more rigorously tested before being bought. Some of them would end up being withdrawn even before the last steam locomotives disappeared. What conformed to a changing policy and looked good on paper failed to live up to the mark.

Just as the Great Western Railway had tried to go it alone with Isambard Kingdom Brunel's 7ft 0¼in broad gauge when everywhere outside its region had adopted George Stephenson's 4ft 8½in standard gauge, so its successor the Western Region chose diesel-hydraulic locomotives as opposed to the diesel-electric types favoured elsewhere. Some of these, like the Class 52 Westerns and Class 42 Warships, turned in very impressive performances, while the North British Locomotive Company's Type 2 Bo-Bos often failed to impress, and had become extinct by 1971. British Railways decided to phase diesel-hydraulics out from the 1960s onwards in pursuit of standardisation, but not before much public money had been wasted. The last Westerns ran in British Rail ownership in 1977.

Needless to say, there are many stories of new diesels failing and having to be rescued by steam engines. Because

The last locomotive built for British Railways was Standard 9F 2-10-0 No. 92220 *Evening Star*, now part of the National Railway Museum collection. NRM

A typical example of a rural branch, the days of which were numbered as rail closures mounted. GWR 0-6-0PT No. 3764 stands at Brecon with a Newport service on November 26, 1962. GREAT WESTERN SOCIETY

Below: **A classic example of an early British Railways diesel railcar is 1956-built Derby lightweight unit M79900, which later became the British Rail Derby research department test coach Iris, is now preserved and restored to as-new condition. It is seen heading a train comprising vintage diesel muiltiple units on the Ecclesbourne Valley Railway in March 2008.**
ROBIN JONES

of the 'one size fits all' policy of phasing out steam, many locomotives which would have been good for several decades, including new BR Standards, were withdrawn and scrapped after only a few years service, to be replaced by inferior diesels.

It has been said that the Modernisation Plan failed because it merely tried to upgrade the existing railway so that it would leap ahead of road transport, rather than looking at the changing needs of customers in a changing world.

Credit: BRITISH RAILWAYS

Steam locomotives were replaced by diesel types on a 'like-for-like' basis: just look at the similarity between the shape of a Class 20 and, say, a large GWR prairie tank. Large numbers of light-duty diesels such as the Class 14s, Class 20s and Class 24s were commissioned for local mixed-goods services, yet those who ordered them failed to see that the days of the pick up goods, where freight wagons were collected from intermediate stations on branch lines and marshalled into one long train, were numbered because of fierce competition from the road hauliers.

In 1954, Britain was one of only seven out of 17 major European countries whose railways were not 'in the red'. The following year, it recorded its first working loss.

The haphazard stab at modernisation that marked the twilight years of steam did not, as everyone was led to believe, improve matters. The annual working deficit in 1956 was £16.5 million: by 1962 it had reached £100 million. Overall, the promised return on investment failed to materialised, the abovementioned Leeds/Barnsley DMU services being one of too few exceptions.

The failure of the Modernisation Plan led to a distrust of British Railways financial planning abilities by the Treasury which was to haunt the nationalised railway for the rest of its existence.

A classic example of a type of diesel hurriedly rushed into production following the British Railways Modernisation Plan was the the Metropolitan-Vickers Co-Bo 1200hp Type B. The first example of the 20-strong class, D5700, broke down several times on its first test run, setting the scene for much of the future of what later became designated Class 28. In March 1959, the 'Metrovicks' were allocated to the overnight London to Glasgow Condor express freight service, but their persistent unreliability eventually led to a decline in demand for the service. On January 4, 1960, 17 out of the 20 were undergoing repairs at Cricklewood Depot, and they were replaced by LMS 'Black Five' 4-6-0s on the Condors.

By 1962, using more reliable diesel types, the Condor service had returned to normal, and after modifications by their manufacturer, the 'Metrovicks' were relegated to local local passenger and freight workings around Barrow-in-Furness. They were finally withdrawn from service in 1968, after just 10 years in traffic, and in the same year that ssteam haulage ended on Bthe national network.

One of them, D5705, has survived for posterity after being kept for use by the Railway Technical Centre at Derby, and later sold into preservation. It is seen on display at Crewe Works during an open weekend in 2005. Incidentally, the type has been immortalised as the character Boco in the Reverend Wilbert Awdry's Thomas the Tank Engine books. ROBIN JONES

The 1950s saw numerous branch line closures well before any rail user had heard the name Beeching. The final train from Gloucester to Lebury is seen arriving at Barbers Bridge behind GWR Collett 0-6-0 No. 3203 on July 11, 1959.
HUGH BALLANTYNE

The balance tips

Many historians who have studied the decline of the British railway network and the switch to road traffic have said that the turning point was not necessarily the poor implementation of modernisation, overdue dieselisation and electrification or growing competition from road hauliers, but the national rail strike of 1955.

During the 1950s, as the austerity years receded and the British economy boomed, trade unions became stronger. Backed by the threat of strike action, unions found themselves able to demand better wages and working conditions for their members.

Days after Anthony Eden's Conservative government won a General Election victory, ASLEF, the Associated Society of Locomotive Engineers and Firemen, the union representing train drivers in Britain, called a strike over a pay dispute. A rise which amounted to around the price of an extra packet of cigarettes a week was demanded.

The strike lasted from May 28 to June 14, and brought British industry to a standstill, although locomen who belonged to the National Union of Railwaymen continued to work. British Railways still managed to convey a quarter of its normal passenger traffic and a third of its freight, but the damage in the minds of the public was irreparable.

The strike signalled a mass switch by both passengers and freight customers from rail to road. They were forced to do so by necessity during the strike, and in a world where road transport was now far more commonplace than ever before, many customers did not return after it ended.

The pick-up goods services were hit hard in the aftermath of the strike. For example, Toddington station on the Stratford-upon-Avon to Cheltenham route, which is now the headquarters of the Gloucestershire Warwickshire Railway, had long been a main centre for the collection of fruit from the orchards of the Vale of Evesham for transportation by rail, mainly to London or the West Midlands. Once the strike was over, the fruit never came back for rail delivery and from then on always went by road, as it does now.

A compromise was eventually reached with the union, but the dispute cost around £12 million in lost revenue. Five years later, the British Transport Commission accepted the findings of a Government-commissioned investigation into railway pay levels, the Guillebaud Report, which led to higher wages and a shorter working week.

However, by then it was too late, for ASLEF had driven a nail into the coffin of the railways as they were.

You cannot blame a union for fighting for better conditions for its members, but by the Fifties there was already widespread condemnation that their leaders were failing to exercise their power responsibly and judiciously. The abuse of power by both management and unions alike was satirised in the 1959 Boulting Brothers comedy film *I'm All Right Jack* starring Peter Sellers, Ian Carmichael and Terry-Thomas.

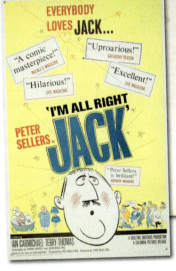

In this instance, the merits of the 1955 national rail strike were questionable: few predicted the severity of the outcome. Trevithick had by necessity turned from roads to rail a century-and-a-half before, but now the balance was clearly and rapidly tipping back again.

The inability of the Modernisation Plan to claw back the promised £85 million a year, coupled with a desire to prevent the country ever being held to ransom again, saw Government transport policy finally shift from rail to road.

A cartoon parody, probably of the 1953 rail strike, accompanied by the caption: "Disgraceful: I bet they do it at Christmas time and prevent my dear wife's mother and father and all her relations coming to stay with us as they always do at the festive season." NRM PICTORIAL COLLECTION

Models like the Coventy-built Triumph Standard 10 helped expand mass car ownership in the 1950s. When the 1955 ASLEF strike meant people had to switch to road, they stayed there afterwards – not because they had to, but because many had found that they could.
ROBIN JONES

Chapter Two

The Marples *master plan*

Minister of Transport Ernest Marples discusses the M1, Britain's first motorway (M1) with Sir Owen Williams, when opening the 72 mile road.
PRESS ASSOCIATION

The October 1959 general election saw the appointment of Ernest Marples as Minister of Transport.

Marples joined the government in 1957 as postmaster general, and introduced the subscriber trunk dialling telephone system which made redundant the use of operators on national telephone calls. He also introduced postcodes to the UK. On June 2, 1957, he started the first draw for the then-new Premium Bonds savings scheme.

He served as transport minister until October 16, 1964, during which time he introduced brought in parking meters, yellow lines and seat belts.

Marples, a qualified accountant, was undeniably a roads man: indeed, he had founded Marples-Ridgway, a construction firm that built many roads, and was to quickly demonstrate that preferred expenditure on motorways to investment in railways. For in 1959, he gave the green light for the first inter-city British motorway, the M1. Britain's first section of motorway, the eight-mile Preston bypass, the first part of the M6 to be completed, was opened on December 5, 1958. It was built after two years of work, without modern hydraulic machinery, and was officially opened by Prime Minister Harold Macmillan, whose car led a convoy along it.

Former bridge engineer Harry Yeadon, 86, later recalled: "People recognised the significance. It was a guinea pig for all the future motorways and a lot of innovation went into its design and construction."

Indeed, it was a massive pointer if there was one, to future national transport trends and policies. Motorways had first been introduced in Italy by Benito Mussolini in the 1920s and then in Germany in 1931, Hitler subsequently speeding up the development programme. In Britain, Lord Montagu had formed a company to build a 'motorway-like road' from London to Birmingham in 1923, but it was not until the Special Roads Act 1949 that the construction of roads limited to vehicle classifications was allowed, and the 1950s when the country's first motorways were given the Government go-ahead.

When the Preston bypass was opened, it had solid shale either side instead of hard shoulders, and if you broke down and tried to change a wheel, the jack sunk into the ground. But it would not remain that way for long.

Happy bedfellows as ancient meets modern – but for how long? LMS Princess Coronation Pacific No. 46242 *City of Glasgow* runs alongside the new M1 near Welton, south of Rugby.
DEREK CROSS/RM

The first section of the M1, between Junction 5 (Watford) and Junction 18 (Crick/Rugby) was opened by Marples on November 2, 1959 in a short ceremony that took place near Slip End, at Junction 10 south of Luton. It has been said that when cars waiting at the Junction to be among the first to travel on the new road poured down the slip road, the recently-appointed transport minister said: "My God, what have I started!"

He expressed concern about cars not been driven in a safe manner, but it was not until 1965 that the 70mph speed limit on motorways was introduced.

To avoid a conflict of interest, Marples undertook to sell his controlling shareholder interest in his road construction company as soon as he became transport minister, although there was a purchaser's requirement that he buy back the shares after he ceased to hold office, at the original price, should the purchaser so require. It was later revealed that he had sold his shares to his wife.

It was therefore ironic that the man who held the future of the railways in his hands should be so closely connected with a major financial interest in road building.

As transport minister, his first move was to impose tighter control over the British Transport Commission and call a halt to the excesses of the modernisation programme.

Early in 1960, the BTC was told that any investment project that involved spending more than £250,000 would have to be cleared with the ministry, the ultimate decision resting with Marples.

By then, there was a widespread feeling at Whitehall that railways were an expensive and increasingly outmoded legacy from Victorian times, and why should the national network be propped up with large amounts of taxpayer's money when roads were being built to do the same job and more effectively?

The slow pruning of the most unprofitable fringes of the railway network had steadily continued throughout the Fifties. In 1953, 275 miles were axed, followed by around 500 miles between 1954-57, and just 150 miles in 1958.

Harold 'Supermac' Macmillan opened Britain's first motorway, the Preston bypass later part of the M6.

Location: Broughton flyover on the M1, near Newport Pagnell (now junction 14) – looking north along the motorway, on October 19, 1959, a fortnight before the road opened. The Automobile Association's special motorway patrol force featuring its new Land Rover and Ford Escort patrol vehicles line up. Above the road is the AA's spotter plane – a de Havilland Dragon Rapide piloted by a former Second World War Mosquito pilot – used to monitor traffic flow and report breakdowns and accidents. AA

Beeching: 55 Years of the Axe Man **21**

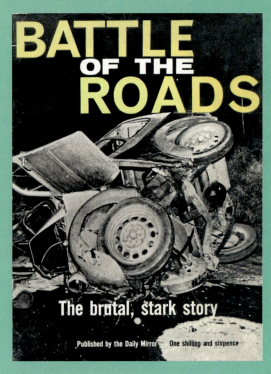

As Transport Minister, Ernest Marples added his name to a *Daily Mirror* one shilling and sixpence booklet packed with horrific pictures of road accidents, as the growth in car ownership and more vehicles on the road led to growing awareness of the huge dangers involved in motoring. It listed the seven deadly signs of the road as impatience, carelessness, selfishness (road hogging), speed, drink, daydreaming and neglect. ROBIN JONES COLLECTION

The British Corporation's stylish small car the Mini brought motoring to within the price range of many ordinary people. The production version of the Mini was demonstrated to the press in April 1959, and by August several thousand cars had been produced ready for the first sales. It became a definitive Sixties icon.

The Ford Zephyr was one of the stylish larger family cars of the early Sixties. ROBIN JONES

The shock to a system

The biggest shock in transport circles came that year, when the closure of a complete system was recommended by a British Railways committee.

On February 28, 1959, the Midland & Great Northern Joint Railway lines closed, apart from a few piecemeal sections like Cromer to Melton Constable. At the Grouping of 1923, the M&GN had been Britain's largest joint railway with 186 route miles, penetrating from the Midlands a junction with the Midland Railway at Saxby into East Anglia where the Great Eastern Railway had otherwise enjoyed a monopoly. It served Great Yarmouth, Norwich and King's Lynn.

The M&GN system was formally operationally incorporated into the LNER in 1936, although it was heavily dependent on the LMS to provide the bulk of its longer-distance traffic including many holiday excursion trains from the Midlands and the north.

Largely single track, in the years following nationalisation it had appeared increasingly vulnerable: a harbinger of doom was the withdrawal of all night goods trains after February 1953.

Early in 1958 there were rumours that closures were on their way, but many were left breathless when the full scale of them became apparent. The whole system was listed among the 350 route miles nationwide to be closed in 1959, the only sections to be left open for passenger traffic were Sheringham to Melton Constable and North Walsham to Mundesley. For the time being, goods trains only were allowed to continue to Rudham from King's Lynn, between Spalding and Bourne, and Spalding and Sutton Bridge.

One reason given was that West Lynn Bridge over the River Great Ouse needed major repairs to its structure, but many saw at the time and still believe today that this was more of an excuse than a reason.

At midnight on February 28, 1959, most of the M&GN system closed. At 8am the following Monday, rail connections at Sutton Bridge were severed and lifting of the track to South Lynn begun in earnest, followed by the demolition of West Lynn Bridge which meant that there could be no going back. The Yarmouth Beach station building was ripped apart, the site becoming a coach station, and by January 1960 the track had been lifted as far as Potter Heigham.

Much of the M&GN rail traffic transferred to former GER lines.

The message to railwaymen was short, sharp and simple: if a complete system could be eradicated overnight, where would the powers-that-be stop in their drive to stem the losses at all costs?

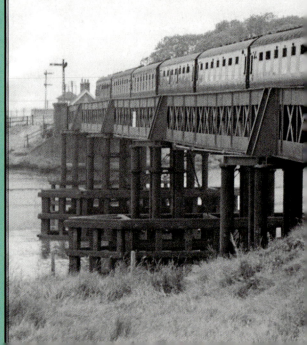

September 1960 sees an AA motorway patrol in full wet weather gear load a broken down car on the hard shoulder of the M1 onto the AA's new 'retriever unit' for recovery on the back of his Land Rover. AA

Pointing the way to the future: at Broughton flyover on the M1, near Newport Pagnell (now junction 14), a senior AA manager appears to be inspecting the new motorway patrol force, outside the organisation's new mobile motorway control centre. AA

It was not only on British Railways where steel wheels had been replaced by rubber tyres. In Britain's cities, the street trams which had brought cheap fast transport in the early 20th century had by then all but been phased out, along with the slightly more versatile trolleybuses that had superseded them in many places.

London's trams ceased operation after July 5, 1952, with Birmingham closing its tramways the following year. The last closure was that of the Glasgow routes on September 2, 1962, leaving only Blackpool with trams. If they could be replaced by buses, why could they not do the job of the railways for people who could not afford a car?

In 1960, one in nine families was said to own a car: that figure seems laughable by today's standards, but, coming three years after Prime Minister Harold Macmillan told Conservative party supporters in Bedford: "Most of our people have never had it so good," it indicated the results of the 1950s wave of prosperity. There were also around 1.9 million motorbikes at the time, again highlighting the prevalence of private transport as an alternative to the railways.

On March 10, 1960, at the start of the parliamentary debate on the above-mentioned Guillebaud Report on railwaymen's wages, Macmillan said: "The carriage of

Last summer: Midland 3F 0-6-0 No 44231 passes the Midland & Great Northern signal bracket as it crosses the River Great Ouse at South Lynn with the 8am Chesterfield to Yarmouth Beach train on August 30, 1958.
HUGH BALLANTYNE

Twenty lay on the route of the Midland & Great Northern Railway line from Saxby and Bourne to Spalding and King's Lynn which closed to passengers in 1959. Nobody knows for sure how the hamlet which grew up in the middle of nowhere around the fenland station got its name: it has been suggested that it was taken from a milestone on the nearby A151 which stated that it was 20 miles to Colsterworth, or it was named after the grid number on an Ordnance Survey map. ROBIN JONES

minerals, including coal, an important traffic for the railways, has gone down. At the same time, there has been an increasing use of road transport in all its forms.

"The industry must be of a size and pattern suited to modern conditions and prospects. In particular, the railway system must be remodelled to meet current needs, and the modernisation plan must be adapted to this new shape.

"Secondly, the public must accept the need for changes in the size and pattern of the industry. This will involve certain sacrifices of convenience, for example, in the reduction of uneconomic services."

His words were music indeed to the ears of the Road Haulage Association, but struck a note that would reverberate throughout the railway industry in the years to come, to the anger of users and staff across the nation.

Yes, cutbacks are needed, but what about subsidies?

Around this time, a report compiled by the Parliamentary Select Committee stated that "there is no doubt that a large-scale British railway system can be profitable".

It emphasised that the size and shape of the system must depend primarily on financial considerations, but Government subsidies for essential but unprofitable services were recommended.

The committee added that direct profitability was not the only consideration. Because of the cost of road building and congestion on them, the national interest may require railway services which do not directly pay for themselves, but which may cost the country less than the alternatives. There are several routes, like the Midland & Great Northern, for which the future may appear to be uncertain, but which might be removed from the "closure list" if such recommendations were adopted.

It was clear, however, that if subsidies are to be paid, the case for their retention must be fully proven, the report said.

Meanwhile, an independent advisory panel chaired by industrialist Sir Ivan Stedeford had been appointed to examine the structure and finances of the British Transport Commission.

Among its members was a Dr Richard Beeching, a physicist and engineer at Imperial Chemical Industries who had been recommended by Sir Frank Smith, ICI's former chief engineer. Following the panel's recommendations, Marples presented a White Paper to Parliament in December 1960, calling for the splitting of the British Transport Commission into a number of bodies, with the railways being run by the new British Railways Board. It also set financial targets for the railways, which would lead to cuts.

The paper read: "Sweeping changes will be needed. Effort and sacrifices will be required from all. The public will have to be prepared to face changes in the extent and nature of the services, provided and, when necessary, in the prices charged for them. The taxpayer will have to face a major capital reorganisation as well as continue to carry a large part of the burden until the railways are paying their way again. Those working in these undertakings, if their livelihood is to be assured, will have to play their part in increasing productivity and enabling the labour force to be deployed so as to secure maximum efficiency.

"The heart of the problem is in the railways. They are a great national enterprise and a vital basic industry. They employ half a million people and represent an investment

The last London tram arrives at New Cross depot on July 5, 1952 packed with passengers. LONDON TRANSPORT MUSEUM/TRANSPORT FOR LONDON

The swing bridge at Sutton Bridge took the Midland & Great Northern Joint Railway across the River Nene. It is still very much in use today as a road bridge carrying the A17. BRIAN SHARPE

of nearly £1600 million, which is growing by more than £100 million each year. A railway system of the right size is an essential element in our transport network and will remain so for as long as can be foreseen. The development of other forms of transport and new techniques now faced British Railways, like the railways in other countries, with problems of competition and adaptation to modern circumstances and public demand.

"The railways are now in a grave financial plight. They are a long way short (by about £60 million a year) of covering even their running costs. This is quite apart from the problem of meeting their interest charges, whether upon the price paid for the undertakings or upon the money since borrowed for modernisation and other purposes. These interest charges now total some £75 million a year.

"The practical test for the railways, as for other transport, is how far the users are prepared to pay economic prices for the services provided. Broadly, this will in the end settle the size and pattern of the railway system. It is already clear that the system must be made more compact. There must also be modernisation, not only of lay-out, equipment and operating methods, but of organisation and management structure."

The break-up of the BTC was facilitated by the Transport Act 1962. Despite brief encouraging figures around the turn of the decade, in 1961 the railways' annual loss on operating account reached nearly £87 million.

On March 15, 1961 Marples told the House of Commons that Dr Richard Beeching would become the first chairman of the new British Railways Board, from June 1 that year.

Mickleover for Radbourn railway station on the Great Northern Railway's Derbyshire Extension lost its regular passenger services in 1939, although excursions lasted until 1959. It was closed in 1964, although the line from Derby Friargate remained in use as a test track by the British Rail Research Division at Derby for several years until the formation was required for road building. MIDLAND RAILWAY TRUST.

Beeching: 55 Years of the Axe Man **25**

Chapter Three

Cometh the hour, cometh the axeman

Few members of the general public had cause to know the name of Richard Beeching until that time.

Beeching was born in Sheerness on the Isle of Sheppey, the second of four brothers. His father was a reporter with the *Kent Messenger*, his mother a schoolteacher and his grandfather on his mother's side a dockyard worker.

Soon after he was born, the Beeching family moved to Maidstone. All four boys attended the local Church of England primary school, Maidstone All Saints, and won scholarships to Maidstone Grammar School. Richard was appointed as a prefect there, although while his three brothers loved cricket, he preferred to go for walks in the countryside.

Richard and Geoffrey Beeching both read physics at London's Imperial College of Science & Technology in London and graduated with first class honours degrees. There, Richard completed a research doctorate under the supervision of Sir George Thomson, the Nobel laureate in physics who achieved fame through his joint discovery of the wave properties of the electron by electron diffraction, and who was knighted in 1943.

Richard Beeching remained in research, taking up a post at London's Fuel Research Station in Greenwich in 1936 and then, the following year, moving to the Mond Nickel Laboratories. There, he became chief physicist, carrying out research in the fields of physics, metallurgy and mechanical engineering.

He married Ella Margaret Tiley in 1938, and the pair set up home in Solihull. The pair had known each other since schooldays.

When he was 29, during the Second World War, Beeching was loaned by Mond Nickel to the Ministry of Supply and worked in the armament design and research departments at Fort Halstead. There, he had a rank equivalent to that of army captain.

He worked under the department's superintendent and chief engineer Sir Frank Smith, the former chief engineer with ICI.

Richard's brother Kenneth was killed in the war.

When Smith returned to ICI after the war, his successor promoted Beeching, now 33, to deputy chief engineer with a rank equivalent to that of brigadier.

Beeching continued his work with armaments, concentrating on anti-aircraft weaponry and small arms, but in 1948 he rejoined his former boss Sir Frank Smith, as his personal technical assistant at ICI.

Zip fasteners not bombs and bullets were now the focus of Beeching's attention. He also worked paints and leather cloth, with a remit to boost efficiency and cut production costs.

During his time at ICI, he was appointed to the Terylene Council, the forerunner of the company's fibres division, the board of which he later joined.

In 1953 he accepted a posting to Canada as vice-president of ICI (Canada) Ltd and was placed in charge of a terylene plant in Ontario.

Dr Richard Beeching leaves Paddington travelling alongside the driver of the train on February 22, 1962. PRESS ASSOCIATION

Dr Beeching on the footplate of GNR 0-6-0 saddle tank No. 1247 during his visit to the Bluebell Railway where he opened a station rather than closed one.
BLUEBELL ARCHIVES

Two years later, he came back to Britain as chairman of the ICI Metals Division on Smith's recommendation.

He was appointed to the ICI board in 1957, serving as technical director, and for a brief period as development director.

It was yet another recommendation by Smith, who had by then retired, that saw Marples appoint Beeching to the previously-mentioned advisory group.

When he was given the job of chairman of British Railways, succeeding Sir Brian Robertson, Beeching was paid an equivalent salary to that which he received at ICI, £24,000 a year, said to be around £370,000 by today's standards. That was £14,000 more than the Prime Minister was paid, and 250 per cent more than the head of any other nationalised industry received at the time. ICI gave Beeching leave of absence for five years by ICI to do the job.

Beeching's brief was simple: return the railways to profitability without delay.

In doing so, he would change the transport map of Britain forever, and for good or bad, create a new streamlined railway system out of the steam era network.

In May 1961, *The Railway Magazine* wrote in its leader column: "The appointment of Dr Beeching has aroused mixed feelings both inside and outside the railway service. Surprise and concern have been expressed because the

Beeching: 55 Years of the Axe Man **27**

The 4½ mile Westerham Valley branch linked Westerham, Brasted and Chevening with Dunton Green and the South Eastern Main Line, a distance of 4½ miles (7.2km). With reported losses of £11,600 per month, British Railways proposed to close it in 1960, but the Central Transport Users' Consultative Committee argued against it. Transport Minister Ernest Marples rejected a petition signed by nearly 2500 residents and it closed on October 28, 1961. A bid by a revivalist group to reopen it along the lines of the Bluebell Railway failed. The trackbed now lies buried under the M25. BRIAN MORRISON

LBSCR 'Terrier' tank engine No 55 *Stepney* passes Ardingly station with two newly-preserved coaches en route to Sheffield Park for the launch of Bluebell Railway passenger services in May 1960. BLUEBELL ARCHIVE

choice did not fall on a senior railway officer who could have brought to the new board many years of specialised experience of the intricacies of railway administration.

"Dr Beeching lacks this qualification, but, as a member of the Stedeford Committee, he must be fully aware of the magnitude of his task. It may be that a man who has attained a high position in the scientific industrial world at a comparatively early age will prove equally successful in the railway sphere, and it would be unfair to prejudge the appointment."

With remarkable clarity of vision, the writer continued: "A noteworthy feature is that Dr Beeching's present intention to return to ICI after five years probably will cause him to be regarded in circles as a surgeon rather than a railwayman."

Ironically, on the same page, it was noted that the first section of the British Transport Commission's museum at Triangle Place, Clapham, London, was opened to the public on Wednesday, March 29. Apart from the then much-smaller York Railway Museum at York, it was the first permanent exhibition in Great Britain entirely devoted to history of transport by rail, road and water. Soon, much much more would be consigned to railway network, not least of all a third of the network.

In his first year in office, while drawing up the legendary blueprint which would bring him overnight fame or notoriety, depending on your perspective, Dr Beeching gained a then-unique insight into at least one controversial railway closure – by helping to reopen it!

On April 1, 1962, he travelled on a railtour from London Bridge via Haywards Heath and Ardingly to Horsted Keynes, where the network still connected with the newly-opened Bluebell Railway, behind Great Northern Railway J52 0-6-0ST No. 1247, the first ex-main line steam engine to be preserved by a private individual. There, he officially opened a new halt built by the Bluebell revivalists in the form of Holywell Halt.

The British Transport Commission had intended to close the loss-making Lewes-East Grinstead line from May 28, 1955. The cross-country route engineered by the London, Brighton & South Coast Railway served mainly rural areas and was largely devoid of passengers, but that did not stop local spinster and battleaxe Madge Bessemer – who normally travelled by private car – launching a campaign to keep it open.

At first she asked for help from the Society for the Reinvigoration of Unremunerative Branch Lines in the United Kingdom, but found the nostalgia-minded organisation to be of less than no practical help.

She then studied key documents from the line's history, and reread the small print in the Act of Parliament which had empowered its building. It required the owners to run four trains each day. Missed by the BTC, she had discovered a loophole.

Helped by local MP Tufton Beamish, she forced the BTC to reinstate the service – very begrudgingly it happened in August the following year. Madge, granddaughter of Henry Bessemer, who invented the process for converting pig iron into steel with his Bessemer Converter, said: "They have to keep the law just like everyone else!"

However, British Railways complied with the letter of the law, but not so much with the spirit of it. While four trains a day were indeed reinstated, they were mostly restricted to just a single coach, and they did not stop at Barcombe or Kingscote, because those two stations did not appear in the original Act of Parliament. Also, the

Above: Doomed before the Beeching era: Melton Mowbray North station lay on the Great Northern Railway & London & North Western Railway joint route from Nottingham (London Road) to Market Harborough, over which regular passenger services ceased on December 7, 1953. However, the lucrative summer specials, mainly from Leicester to Skegness or Mablethorpe, survived until 1962, and through goods traffic lasted until 1964. Ivatt mogul No. 43066 carries a wreath on its tender on the line's last day, July 5, 1964.
R BIDDICK/COLOUR-RAIL.COM

A British Railways delivery truck in London in 1962. One of Beeching's biggest tasks was to make rail freight pay.
DON O'BRIEN/CREATIVE COMMONS

Beeching: 55 Years of the Axe Man **29**

Not exactly the Beeching Axe of legend: Dr Beeching never had a physical axe as such but he did start off with a pair of scissors, preserved in the National Railway Museum at York. These scissors were made to mark the opening of the rebuilt Plymouth station opened by him on March 26, 1962. They were made by T Hardy & Sons that same year and were donated to the NRM by Beeching's daughter Ann Bailey. NRM

services appeared to be deliberately timed so that they would be of little use – arriving at East Grinstead after the start of normal working hours and leaving before knocking-off time.

The 'Sulky Service', as it came to be nicknamed, kept the line alive while British Railways went to the time and trouble to obtain the necessary statutory powers for revoking the terms of the original Act.

Services were again withdrawn between Lewes and East Grinstead on March 16, 1958, but Madge Bessemer had by then attracted the ears of the national press, radio and TV to her cause. When the final train ran, the unduly large numbers of passengers and sightseers proved that the public at large really did care about rail closures.

On that last day, Madge met Chris Campbell, a part-time student at Carshalton Technical College who had many recollections of travelling on the line while spending school holidays with relatives. Inspired by her efforts to save the line, Chris, 18, wondered if there was anything that could still be done. Elsewhere, Martin Eastland, 19, a telecommunications engineering student of Haywards Heath, David Dallimore, a student at the London School of Economics, from Woodingdean, and Brighton-based Alan Sturt, 19, who was studying at the Regent Street Polytechnic, had kicked around the idea of setting up a Lewes and East Grinstead Railway Preservation Society.

The publicity machine was sparked off again in December 1958 by a chance remark made by Chris to a reporter on the *East Grinstead Observer* about the formation of the preservation society, leading to the headline: "Bluebell Line Sensation – May Be Run Privately".

Chris travelled on a Rambler's Excursion from London Victoria to Horsted Keynes on December 7, two days after the report appeared. At Horsted Keynes, his party of 15 walked south along the disused trackbed to Newick & Chailey station where they had lunch in view of Madge who was picking flowers on the lineside opposite. It was then that Chris met Martin for the first time and decided to call a public meeting to officially launch the society.

The landmark founders' meeting was held on March 15, 1959, at the Church Lads Brigade Hall in Haywards Heath. It was chaired by one Bernard Holden because the students, all under 21, were minors in the eyes of the then law and legally barred from holding positions. Bernard, 51, a signalling assistant in the general manager's office at Liverpool Street, had been born in Barcombe station house where his father Charles was stationmaster.

The rest is history. Part of the line, between Sheffield Park and a point south of Horsted Keynes, reopened on August 7, 1960. The revivalists did not succeed in their original ambition to save the entire Lewes-East Grinstead route, but their Bluebell Railway slowly but surely grew to become a market leader in preserved steam railways.

There would be many more would-be Madge Bessemers in the decade that followed, but few would meet with even a hint of her albeit temporary success in the face of an unprecedented tidal wave of Whitehall negativity against rural railways.

As for Dr Beeching, he and his wife moved to nearby East Grinstead in the Sixties and he spent the rest of his life there.

Ironically, Holywell Halt subsequently closed while the Bluebell Railway thrives!

The quadrangle at Maidstone Grammar School which Richard Beeching attended. THE MAIDSTONIAN

Oh Mr Porter

In late 1962, Beeching, answering a question about railway porters' manners, told the annual conference of the Institute of Directors: "The porters are among the lowest-paid grades on the railways. We do not therefore have great freedom of choice and do have a very considerable turnover.

"So the porter whom you ask 'where does the 6.15 to somewhere go?' has only been there a fortnight himself and might equally ask you.

"Many porters are extremely polite and extremely patient. Others are not. The ratio is much the same among the passengers."

Dr Beeching was not responsible for the replacement of steam locomotives, but he certainly speeded up their demise. Among the potential replacements was the English Electric's experimental gas turbine-mechanical 4-6-0 which appeared in early 1961, looking far more like a steam engine than a diesel, and was based somewhat on a Class 5 steam design. The culmination of 15 years' design work, it impressed in trials in Shropshire, North Wales, on the Great Central main line and over Shap, but was found to be high on fuel consumption, and its reversing mechanism was inadequate. Sadly, it was not saved for posterity but was scrapped in early 1966. RM

Left: The writing had been on the wall for the heavily lossmaking Midland & South Western Junction Railway from Cheltenham to Andover since nationalisation, and the end came on September 10, 1961, three months after Beeching's appointment, but arranged before his arrival. The Stephenson Locomotive Society ran the last passenger train, a special on September 10, 1961, behind GWR 4-6-0 No. 7808 *Cookham Manor*.
D LOVELOCK/RM

Left & above: GWR prairie tank No. 4178 climbs from Lightmoor Junction to Doseley Halt with the 7.05pm from Much Wenlock, the last passenger train on the latter branch, on July 21, 1962. Three years later and long devoid of track, Much Wenlock station was a typical Beeching era ruin.
W A CAMWELL/RM P B TAYLOR/RM

Chapter Four

The times they are a-changing

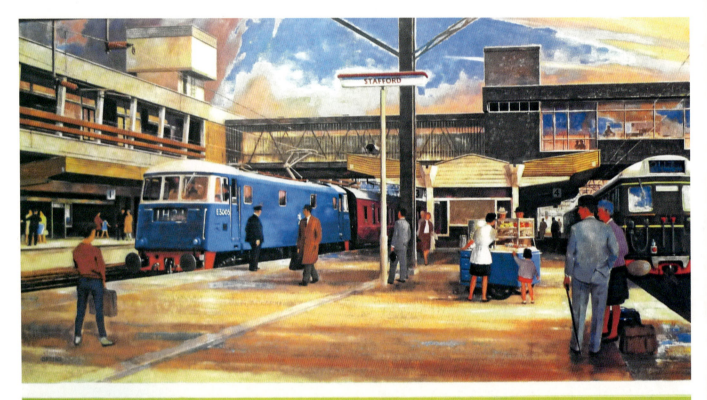

Above: **Poster promoting the new electric services on the West Coast Main Line.** BRITISH RAILWAYS/NRM

So life was never better than
In nineteen sixty-three
(Though just too late for me) –
Between the end of the Chatterley ban
And the Beatles' first LP.
So ran the final verse of Philip Larkin's poem *Annus Mirabilis*, which homed in on the beginnings of arguably what might well be considered the greatest decade of change in the history of western civilisation, one in which everything that went before would be reassessed and if found wanting, replaced. Everything, it seemed, was up for grabs in a new supersonic age promising unparalleled technical progress and personal liberty.

Few saw it coming, although maybe they should have learned the lessons of the aftermath of the First World War and the 'lost generation', the youngsters who came of age during the conflict and who were afterwards determined that there would be no return to the old order.

As the gloom lifted from Britain with the passing of the years of austerity, with its ration books, shortage and National Service, there abound a new-found affluence and with it a sense of freedom, which began with a yearning and evolved into demands and insistence.

Maybe better education of the masses played a liberating part, or perhaps it was the higher wages and better working conditions that the Fifties ushered in, or the advance of popular technology. The Fifties brought TV into many people's homes for the first time, and while at first viewers' diet was limited to the BBC, the 'voice of the establishment', the emergence of ITV, the commercial channel funded by advertising and which could afford to pay the big stars of stage and screen to appear, bringing them into ordinary homes for the first time.

Then there was rock 'n' roll

The 1955 social commentary film *Blackboard Jungle*, about teachers and unruly pupils in an inner-city school, sparked off a teenage revolution by itself. The film is best known for the single by Bill Haley & His Comets, *Rock Around the Clock*, which became an overnight hit and stayed at the top of the Billboard charters for eight weeks.

When shown at a cinema near the Elephant and Castle in south London in 1956 the teenage teddy boy audience started to rip up seats and dance in the aisles. Their actions sparked off a trend, with copycat riots taking place in cinemas around Britain wherever the film was shown. While the vandalism died down after a few months, *Blackboard Jungle* is viewed by many historians as the beginning of a period of visible teenage rebellion in the late 20th century, in which what was seen as the 'old order' was there to also be ripped up and torn down.

While Haley, who had started his career as a country and western singer, was quickly superseded as a teenage icon by the likes of Elvis Presley, Little Richard, Chuck Berry and Eddie Cochran, and in Britain, Cliff Richard and the Shadows, Lonnie Donegan and Tommy Steele, a rolling stone had been set in motion that, with the aid of Beatlemania in 1963, a fateful year for both Larkin and the railways, became an unstoppable social and cultural revolution.

The old order was also on its way out in the world of literature and censorship. The ban on D H Lawrence's novel *Lady Chatterley's Lover* ended in 1960 with an obscenity trial at the Old Bailey, when Penguin Books was prosecuted under an Act of Parliament introduced in 1959. This law made it possible for publishers to avoid conviction if they could show that a work was of literary merit.

With *Lady Chatterley*, one of the principal objections was the use of the 'f-word'. Chief prosecutor Mervyn Griffith-Jones, however, scored a major own goal when he asked the jury if it were the kind of book "you would wish your wife or servants to read". By then, how many ordinary people kept servants? Was there one law for the middle and upper classes and another for everyone else?

Compare the publicity over the trial with the secrecy and deafening silence which was dished out to the British public during the Edward VIII abdication crisis in 1936. No details of the newly-crowned king appeared in the British press while it was in full swing, thanks to the firm control of the newspapers by the establishment, yet at the same time every lucid detail appeared in the press on the far side of

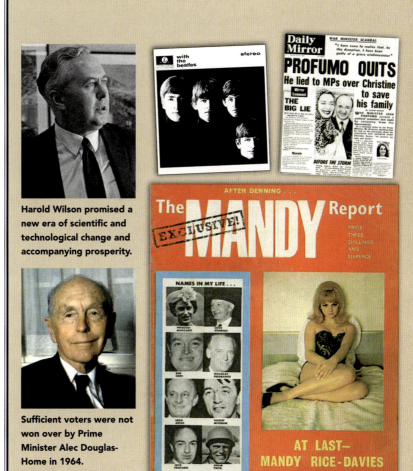

Harold Wilson promised a new era of scientific and technological change and accompanying prosperity.

Sufficient voters were not won over by Prime Minister Alec Douglas-Home in 1964.
ALLAN WARREN/ CREATIVE COMMONS

the Atlantic. It was only when Edward VIII announced his abdication so he could marry Mrs Simpson, as portrayed in the 2011 multiple award-winning film *The King's Speech*, that we Brits were permitted to know the basics of what had really been going on regarding our monarchy.

The *Chatterley* jury of three women and nine men returned a verdict of not guilty on November 2, 1960, making the novel available for the first time to the British public. It has now long since been considered a literary masterpiece.

Walls came tumbling down in the field of politics. Sir Harold Macmillan, the British Prime Minister, who seemed to epitomise the status quo of the old establishment, resigned on the grounds of ill health a medical misdiagnosis on October 18, 1963, during the Conservative Party conference. In its final year, the credibility of his government had been permanently damaged by the Profumo affair. John Profumo, Secretary of State for War, had lied to the House of Commons about his affair with Christine Keeler, the reputed mistress of an alleged Russian spy.

To the rebellious youth of the time, the scandal appeared to represent the moral decay of the British establishment. Years later, I was told by journalists that the exposure of the affair by the British press was revenge for a 'D-notice' (gagging order) used to suppress revelations about a senior aristocrat and his relationship with a soldier.

Indeed, in several ways it highlighted a new-found freedom of the press in the early Sixties' winds of change. Incidentally, homosexuality between men aged 21 and over was decriminalised in England and Wales under the Sexual Offences Act 1967, one of many more benchmarks in the sexual revolution that popularly typifies the Sixties.

Following the resignation of 'Supermac', the Conservatives demonstrated that they 'just did not get it' as far as the mood of the public was concerned. They liked and wanted change and fast, but despite multi-dimensional moves away from what had gone before, the surprise successor to Macmillan was simply more of the same… and visibly so.

Foreign Secretary Alec Douglas-Home took over as prime minister: known as The Earl of Home from 1951 to 1963 after he inherited his father's peerage, he gave it up to move from the Lords to accept the position of Prime Minister, using the Peerage Act 1963, which had been passed earlier to allow Tony Benn to disclaim his peerage as Lord Stansgate. The old wine was repackaged as Sir Alec Douglas-Home, and in his new identity he won a by-election in the safe seat of Kinross & West Perthshire so he could enter the Commons.

The Profumo affair had, however, so badly tarnished the Conservative Government that it was incapable of being saved, least of all by a 60-year-old aristocrat who in the view of the general public represented much of the past that they wanted rid of. By contrast, the Labour party was newly led in 1963 by Harold Wilson, a comparative youngster at 46.

At the Labour Party's annual conference that year, Wilson delivered a keynote on the implications of scientific and technological change, stating that "the Britain that is going to be forged in the white heat of this revolution will be no place for restrictive practices or for outdated measures on either side of industry".

In short, he promised a way forward into a new age of achievement and prosperity, one unshackled to the prevailing class system that was licking its wounds from the Profumo scandal.

Thirteen years of Conservative rule ended when Labour won the 1964 general election by just four seats, taking Wilson into No 10 Downing Street, and seeking a bigger majority after 18 months, a second election in March 1966 returned Wilson 96 seats clear of his rivals.

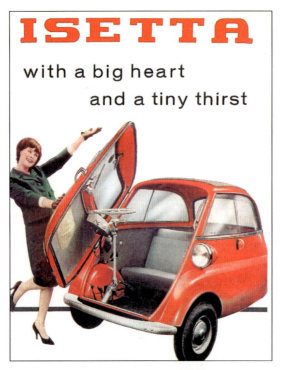

To quote a classic Beatles album track, the motor car was getting here, there and everywhere in the early Sixties. If you wanted a brand new budget motor, you could opt for a bubble car, a three-wheeler based around motorcycle technology, while the more adventurous could opt for an Amphicar, which claimed to be equally at home on land or in the water, and could be used as a motorboat. ROBIN JONES COLLECTION

Britain's only hovertrain, RTV31, is preserved at Railworld. ROBIN JONES

The prototype hovertrain test track at Earith near Cambridge in 1972. RAILWORLD

The world's first hovercraft, Saunders-Roe Nautical 1, inspired the development of hovertrain technology in Britain.

Transport for the space age

Change was everywhere. City dwellers saw mass clearances of slums during the Fifties and Sixties, and the erection of new estates and high-rise tower blocks on green field sites to replace them, although successive generations would challenge whether these had brought about a marked improvement in social conditions for their working class inhabitants. Town centres were redesigned: many old small shops were swept away for new department stores, as brushed concrete replaced Victorian red bricks.

Car ownership soared during the Sixties, and this by itself gave the individual the freedom to choose where they went, no longer limited to railway lines or bus routes.

At the other extreme of the modern transport spectrum, the Russian cosmonaut Yuri Alekseyevich Gagarin became the first human to venture into outer space, on April 12, 1961, setting the stage for the Cold War race to the moon which was won by the USA when Apollo 11's lunar module touched down in the Sea of Tranquility on July 20, 1969, Commander Neil Armstrong and pilot 'Buzz' Aldrin setting foot on the surface the following day.

The concept of a space age had featured heavily in popular movies and sci-fi TV series during the Fifties and Sixties: it was widely seen as the new frontier in which imagination was the only limiting factor, and there were many who sincerely believed we would be making missions to Mars and maybe beyond by the end of the century.

Space rockets were not the only futuristic forms of travel being developed.

On the Isle of Wight, an island since the last ice age, parliamentary powers for a railway tunnel beneath the Solent were obtained in 1901. The scheme failed to raise sufficient capital, was briefly revived after the First World War, but ultimately came to nothing.

Yet why build a railway under the sea if you can go almost as quickly over it?

On June 11, 1959, aero and marine engineering company and flying boat builder Saunders-Roe Limited, based at Columbine Works in East Cowes, demonstrated the Saunders-Roe Nautical 1 (SR-N1), the first hovercraft built to inventor Christopher Cockerell's design, under contract to the National Research and Development Corporation. A fortnight later, it crossed the English Channel from Calais to Dover.

The firm went on to develop more hovercraft, including the SR-N2, which began operations over the Solent in 1962, and the ASR-N6, which ran from Southsea to Ryde for several years.

Above: Seaspeed was the hovercraft division of British Rail. Established in 1965, it started its first service in 1966. It began cross-Channel services from Dover to Calais and Boulogne-sur-Mer in 1968 using SR-N4 hovercraft *The Princess Margaret*, which featured in the James Bond film *Diamonds Are Forever*, and *The Princess Anne*. The service ended in 2000 and both are preserved at the Hovercraft Museum in Lee-on-the-Solent, Hampshire. FRAMMY7/CREATIVE COMMONS

Beeching: 55 Years of the Axe Man **35**

Incidentally, a site on High Down near the Needles Battery, tested Black Knight and Black Arrow rocket engines for the British intercontinental ballistic missile programme between 1956-71. The rockets later launched the Prosper X3 satellite, the only one successfully launched by a British rocket, from Woomera in Australia on October 28, 1971.

The hovercraft was widely seen as a great step forward, some believing it could do for transport in the 20th century what the steam locomotive had done in the 19th. In the wake of the success of the early hovercraft, inventors set to work adapting the air-cushion principle to land transport, including railways. Visions of futuristic monorails so often portrayed in the boys' comics of the day pointed to an era in which steam, diesel and electric locomotives, indeed anything that ran on two rails, would be yesterday's traction.

Air cushion technology offered lower frictional forces and therefore in theory could produce high speeds. The hovertrain concept was devised by English engineer Professor Eric Laithwaite of Imperial College, London, who experimented with linear induction motors and produced the first full-size working model of such a motor in the late Forties.

Paving the way in this field of research was the Aérotrain, an experimental high-speed hovertrain built and operated in France between 1965 and 1977.

In England, a short test track for a tracked hovercraft rail system was constructed by Tracked Hovercraft Ltd at Earith near Cambridge, sandwiched between two of the fenland's biggest drains, the Old Bedford River and the Counter Drain.

Funded by the Government, a test vehicle, RTV31, was built. It was fitted with linear magnetic motors for forward motion, while a cushion of air powered from giant fans raised the vehicle off the track.

It reached 104mph from a standing start over a mile on February 7, 1973 – only for the project funding to be cancelled a week later by Aerospace Minister, Michael Heseltine, after it was considered to be too expensive for commercial use. Engineering firm Alfred McAlpine took over parts of the project, but it was finally abandoned in the mid Eighties. No, it would not become the preferred transport of the brave new world of the Sixties' technocrat visionaries, but a static exhibit outside Peterborough's Railworld museum, and as far as this technology was concerned, Mars would have to wait.

CHANNEL TUNNEL
The Channel Tunnel exhibit in the Great Hall at the National Railway Museum at York.
EXTREME MACHINE UK/CREATIVE COMMONS

Below the waves

Mankind was not only reaching for the sky and beyond in the Sixties, we were also planning to take public transport beneath the sea.

On February 6, 1964, the British and French governments agreed a deal for the construction of a Channel Tunnel. The twin-tunnelled rail link between Britain and the continent, linking the two physically for the first time since the last ice age, would take five years, it was announced.

Unlike hovercraft and hovertrains, a Channel Tunnel was not a new idea, and had been first seriously mooted in 1802, only to repeatedly fall foul over concerns about British national security being compromised. However, in 1955, the defence argument was accepted to be no longer relevant because of the superiority of air power.

Despite the agreement, work on building the tunnel did not start for another decade, and was cancelled in January 1975 to the dismay of the French after Harold Wilson was returned to power.

Another agreement, the Treaty of Canterbury, was signed in February 1986 and work began again in 1988, the tunnel opening in 1994.

36 Beeching: 55 Years of the Axe Man

Diesel and electric trains for the future

British Railways did, however, have one big futuristic trick up its sleeve, one that certainly inspired the imagination in a world in which the public was being told that steam was on the way out.

The iconic Blue Pullman came off the drawing board in the late 1950s, underwent its trials before the turn of the decade, and was then unleashed on the Birmingham Snow Hill-Paddington line, as well as on the Midland route to Manchester.

Branded with the classic Pullman hallmark of utmost quality, the new diesel trains offered meals at every seat, air conditioning, and a staffing level good enough to ensure that passengers would want for nothing. Indeed, it looked more towards the comforts and style associated with aircraft than traditional railway carriages.

A smoothness of ride was also assured by an all-new design of coach.

As steam engines dwindled and more diesels appeared, the eight-carriage Blue Pullmans was certainly a star turn for the hordes of schoolboy locospotters on the lineside. However, their admiration was not always shared by those on board, who found out that looks were not everything – as many complained of a very bumpy ride.

When British Rail chose the London Midland Region's Euston-Birmingham New Street line, part of the West Coast Main Line, into the primary route between Britain's two biggest cities, as opposed to the Western Region's rival Paddington-Birmingham Snow Hill line, and electrify it, the Blue Pullman's days were numbered. The former Paddington line was downgraded to a secondary route, and the Pullmans were despatched to the less lucrative Bristol and Cardiff routes. They were all withdrawn by 1973, and not one coach was saved for preservation, and no, they did not persuade sufficient car owners to switch back to rail travel as had been originally hoped.

By contrast, one of the biggest linear developments following the 1955 Modernisation Plan was the 25kV electrification of the West Coast Main Line from Euston to Glasgow, completed in stages between 1959 and 1974, the first length, Crewe to Manchester, completed on September 12, 1960, followed by Crewe to Liverpool, completed on January 1, 1962. The first electric trains from London ran on November 12, 1965.

Electrification of the Birmingham line was completed on March 6, 1967.

Once electrification was complete between London, the West Midlands and the North West, new high-speed long-distance services were introduced in 1966, launching British Rail's highly successful Inter-City brand. This

Above: West Coast Main Line electrics were viewed at British Railway's flagship produce in the mid Sixties. AL1 electric locomotive E3017 and AL5 E3089 approach Rugby with the up 'Ulster Express' on December 28, 1964. BRIAN HICKS

Luxury table service in a Blue Pullman saloon. BRITISH RAILWAYS

Beeching: 55 Years of the Axe Man **37**

innovation brought hitherto-unknown journey times such as London to Manchester or Liverpool in 2 hours 30 minutes for the twice-daily Manchester Pullman. Services ran hourly to Birmingham and two-hourly to Manchester.

We often look back at the Sixties as a period whereby the public regretted the passing of steam trains in favour of modern traction. However, in the build-up to the launch of electric services from London to the West Midlands, Liverpool and Manchester in late 1966, British Rail produced souvenir items as part of a publicity drive.

Within a few weeks of going on sale, practically the whole stock of 50,000 penny blue and white 'London Midland Express' lapel badges were sold. Coloured blue and white, they were introduced to publicise the Euston-Liverpool-Manchester electrified services. Shoulder travel bags, bearing the legend 'Inter-City Electric; and on sale at principal stations for 15 shillings, also proved popular.

So successful was the public response to the London Midland Region electrification exhibition train that it was taken on tour to the Southern Region, where third-rail electric on commuter lines from London has been the norm for decades.

Along with electrification came the gradual introduction of modern British Rail coaches such as the Mark 2 and, following the northern electrification scheme's completion in 1974, the air-conditioned Mark 3s.

These carriages remained the mainstay of West Coast Main Line express services until the early 21st century.

On the route, line speeds were raised to a maximum 110mph. Hauled by Class 86 and Class 87 electric locomotives, the West Coast Main Line services were viewed as the nationalised railway's flagship passenger product, having the effect of doubling traffic between 1962 and 1975 after years of stagnation. This proved that if the public was given the right product, in the right

location, and backed by sufficient capital investment, the railways' fortunes could be reversed.

The electrification of the route was accompanied by the total redevelopment of the Victorian stations along it and replaced with Sixties designs built from glass and concrete, and lacking much of the ornamentation and style of their predecessors, placing functionality first. The redevelopment of Euston went as far as demolishing the famous Doric Arch entrance portal despite widespread opposition. Coventry, Birmingham New Street, Stafford and Manchester Piccadilly were, for better or worse, rebuilt.

However, by contrast, the Blue Pullmans, they were like so much in the Sixties, promising the earth yet ultimately delivering comparatively little that they had promised, although in fairness, lessons learned from their design paved the way for the introduction of the Inter-City 125 High Speed Trains in the seventies, and these were so successful that they are still with us now.

Larkin's poem quoted earlier talked about: "A brilliant breaking of the bank, A quite unlosable game", and so it was in the Sixties, when it seemed that nothing could halt the march of progress, with innovation and invention lurking around every corner to surprise and delight us. Yet much of the optimism and positivety surrounding the era, or at least our popular image of it, ultimately turned out to be out of sync with reality, and failed to fully predict the medium and long-term implications of change that too often rushed off the drawing board and way ahead of itself.

It was in this most fertile of decades that one man, empowered by the Government, would front a series of ground-shifting and hugely-controversial decisions that he believed would finally yank Britain's entire national railway network out of the age of the Big Four so it would serve the needs of the times in which 'liberated' mankind would take his first giant steps on the moon.

A Western Region Blue Pullman set on Hatton bank between Birmingham Snow Hill and Leamington in 1966. It was introduced in a bid to make rail travel fashionable again.
MICHAEL MENSING

Chapter Five

The Reshaping of *British Railways*

Dr Richard Beeching holds up a copy of his 1963 report, *The Reshaping of British Railways*. NRM

Above: **The Cambrian Railways' Mid-Wales line linked Newtown, Llanidloes, Rhayader, Builth Wells and Brecon and had more than 20 intermediate stations serving sparse local populations. It closed on December 31, 1962. Ivatt 2-6-0 No. 46523 is seen arriving at Llanidloes with the 5.40pm Moat Lane Junction to Builth Wells on June 7, 1960. Cars won the day here: the site is now occupied by the town's bypass.**
HUGH BALLANTYNE

The Transport Act 1962, which broke up the British Transport Commission and created the British Railways Board, set the scene for what was to quickly follow. The new board was directed under Section 22 of the Act to run the railways so that its operating profits were "not less than sufficient" for meeting the running costs.

This clause marked a major first for British railway legislation and was a turning point for the system, for from then onwards, each railway service should pay for itself or at least show that it had the possibility of doing so. The days of mass subsidy, with profitable services supporting the unprofitable ones, and the taxpayer footing the bill if the overall figures did not tally in the right way, would soon be over, or so it was intended.

It was the Select Committee of the House of Commons on Nationalised Industries which had decided that the British Transport Commission should make its decisions exclusively on considerations of "direct profitability". Where decisions not based on self-sufficiency but "on grounds of the national economy or of social needs" had to be taken, the Minister of Transport would shoulder the responsibility.

No longer would there be a special case for the railways: they would have to compete in a free market in the same way as any other business. Section 3(1) of the Act stated that it was the duty of the British Railways Board to provide railway services with regard to "efficiency, economy and safety of operation".

The 1962 Act also introduced new legislation for the closure of railway lines. Section 56(7) demanded that British Railways gave at least six weeks notice of its intention to close a line and to publish the proposal in two local newspapers in the area affected in two successive weeks.

Each notice would have to provide the proposed closure dates, details of alternative public transport, including services which British Railways was to lay on as a result of closure and inviting objections within the six week period to a specified address.

A copy of the notice was also to be sent to the relevant Area Transport Users Consultative Committee, which would receive objections from affected rail users, and submit a report to the Minister of Transport.

The Central Transport Consultative Committee was a new body that replaced a similar one established under the Transport Act 1947 which nationalised the railways, and was intended to represent the railways' consumers. The Area

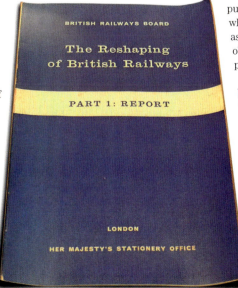

Left: **Dr Beeching's report *The Reshaping of British Railways*, a key document in British railway history on display in the National Railway Museum at York.**
ROBIN JONES

Beeching: 55 Years of the Axe Man **41**

In a scene typical of Beeching closures and final trains, hordes of lineside photographers scramble to take a picture of Ivatt 2-6-2T No. 41222 leaving Wolverton on September 5, 1964, the last day of service on the Newport Pagnell branch.
K FAIREY/COLOUR-RAIL.COM

Transport Users Consultative Committees were additional bodies set up to cover local areas.

It would be the job of the Area Committees to look at the hardship which it considered would be caused as a result of the closure, and recommend measures to ease that hardship.

The line closure would not go ahead until the Area Committee had reported to the transport minister and he had given his consent to it. Based on the Area Committee's report, the minister could subject his consent to closure to certain conditions, such as the provision of alternative transport services. However, the minister was not bound to follow any of the Area Committee's recommendations, and therefore there was no safeguard by which public feeling would take priority over policy.

In December 1962, *The Railway Magazine* reported: "The name of Dr Beeching is likely to live on in the Leicestershire village of Countesthorpe long after the current railway troubles are forgotten. It is reported that the parish council there has agreed to name a new thoroughfare off Station Road 'Beeching Close' because residents associate him with the closure of their railway station.

Countesthorpe station, just south of Leicester on the Midland line to Rugby, had closed in February 1962. While villagers there might have been irate, they would soon have likeminded bedfellows – to the tune of many millions. The nation had not seen anything yet.

The doctor prescribes the medicine

The biggest shock to the railway system was delivered on March 27, 1963, when Dr Beeching's report, *The Reshaping of British Railways*, was published. Seasoned railwaymen had seen traffic dwindle to a trickle or nothing on many lines and knew that closures were inevitable; however, the publication of a report detailing sweeping changes of the extent proposed was still received by many with horror.

To members of the ordinary public, who had no grasp of railway finances, and had always accepted that the railways 'would always be there', Beeching would be immortalised as the man who took 'their' line away.

Dubbed the 'Beeching Bombshell' or the 'Beeching Axe' by the press, the 148 page report called for a third of the rail network to be closed and ripped up.

Out of around 18,000 route miles, 5000, mainly comprising cross-country routes and rural branches, should close completely, it recommended.

Not only were branches to rural backwaters listed for closure: this time, trunk routes were listed – the Somerset & Dorset Joint Railway system, the Waverley Route from Carlisle to Edinburgh, the Great Central Railway from Nottingham to Marylebone, along with passenger

Above: **A scene soon to be repeated all over Britain: Pye Hill & Somercotes station on the Great Northern Railway's Pinxton branch in Nottinghamshire, which closed on January 1, 1963.** MIDLAND RAILWAY TRUST

Left: **Last man standing: a lone explorer examines the ruins of Pye Hill & Somercotes station.** MIDLAND RAILWAY TRUST

services on the Settle and Carlisle route.

Over and above all this, many other lines were to lose their passenger services and remain open for freight only, while intermediate stations serving small communities on main lines should close, with the aim of speeding up inter-city trains. A total of 2363 stations and halts were to be closed, including 435 under consideration before the report appeared, of which 235 had already been closed.

The proposed mass changes to the network would be implemented in a seven-year programme, the report recommended.

Basically, the report said that railways should be used to meet that part of the national transport requirement for which they offered the best available means, and stop trying to compete in areas where they were now ill-suited.

The report followed a key study initiated by Beeching into traffic flows on all the railway routes in the country.

This study, which had been carried out during the week ending April 23, 1962, two weeks after Easter, found that 30% of route miles carried just 1% of passengers and freight, and half of all stations contributed just 2% of income.

Half the total route mileage carried about 4% of the total passenger miles, and around 5% of the freight ton miles, revenue from them amounting to £20 million with the costs double that figure. Clearly, the figures did not stack up, nor, it seemed, were ever likely to again.

From the least-used half of the stations the gross revenue from all traffic did not even cover the cost of the stations themselves, and made no contribution to route costs, movement or terminal costs.

Regarding branch lines, figures showed it was doubtful if the revenue from up to 6000 passengers a week covered movement costs alone, and clearly money would be saved by withdrawing the service.

The report stated that overall, passenger traffic on a single-track branch line added around £1750 a mile to

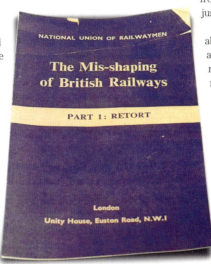

Left: **The National Union of Railwaymen's response to Beeching's report. It was titled The Mis-Shaping of Britain's Railways.** ROBIN JONES

Beeching: 55 Years of the Axe Man **43**

Above: **Collett auto tank No. 1453 and trailer W244W moves off from Sharpness with the 4.15pm service to Berkeley road on September 26, 1964. The Sharpness branch closed to passengers in November 1964 and goods in January 1966, but the line serving Sharpness Docks was retained, and is now being revived by enthusiasts as the Berkeley Vale Railway.**
HUGH BALLANTYNE

Below: **The last train on Hertfordshire's 13.8 mile Buntingford branch, the 9.45am diesel multiple unit service to St Margarets, at Hadham on November 14, 1964.**
HUGH BALLANTYNE

the cost of route maintenance, signalling and the staffing of stations.

Therefore, a passenger density below 10,000 could not be considered as economic, even where freight traffic absorbed a proportion of the route cost.

Where there was no other traffic, 17,000 passengers per week might make a branch line pay its way.

Even the provision of railbuses – a cost-cutting measure introduced on many branches in the late Fifties as a key element of a drive to prune staffing levels and increase efficiency – demanded a passenger density of 14,000 a week, as against 17,000 a week with diesel multiple units.

Beeching stated in the opening to his report that "there had never before been any systematic assembly of a basis of information upon which planning could be founded, and without which the proper role of the railways in the transport system as a whole could not be determined".

Taken at face value, that claimed it was the first time that a detailed study of the economy of the nation's railways as a whole had been attempted, rather than the individual regions of British Railways (Western, London Midland, Eastern, Southern and Scottish) largely doing their own thing. Maybe if such a nationwide study had been attempted as part of the implementation of the Modernisation Plan, it would not have been implemented in such a haphazard, localised and floundering manner.

The report read: "Throughout these investigations and the preparation of this report the British Railways Board has had it in mind that its duty is to employ the assets vested in it, and develop or modify them, to the best advantage of the nation."

As we have seen, Beeching did not invent rail closures: a steady process of eliminating non-remunerative lines had been underway for decades. Indeed, several of the routes listed in The Reshaping of British Railways had already been proposed for closure by their regions: Beeching merely confirmed those decisions.

The closures of poorly-used lines had fallen from 350 in 1959 to 175 in 1960, and even further to 150 in 1961. Yet in 1962, the year before *The Reshaping of British Railways* appeared, they shot up to 780. The Western Region, for one, which had embraced dieselisation, was making much publicity out of the improvements it was making, after years of closing branches serving rural backwaters.

In 1963, before the newly-recommended Beeching closures could be implemented, 324 miles were axed.

By taking a global view and applying the same criteria to all regions across the country, Beeching may be seen as merely streamlining the decision-making processes that had gone before, with a universal set of criteria. Not only that, it was Marples who employed him and instructed him – the doctor was "only obeying orders".

Much of the report proposed that British Rail electrify some trunk routes and eliminate uneconomic wagon-load traffic in favour of containerised freight traffic.

The report – which claimed that the measures should eradicate the railways' deficit by 1970 – automatically sparked immediate outrage from many of the communities which would become disenfranchised by the rail network as a result of the closures.

However, the Conservative Government, which accepted Beeching's report after it was debated in the House of Commons in April 1963, promised that axed rail services would be replaced by bus services, which would be much cheaper to operate.

The report said: "Today, rail stopping services and bus services serve the same basic purpose. Buses carry the greater part of the passengers moving by public transport in rural areas, and, as well as competing with each other,

44 Beeching: 55 Years of the Axe Man

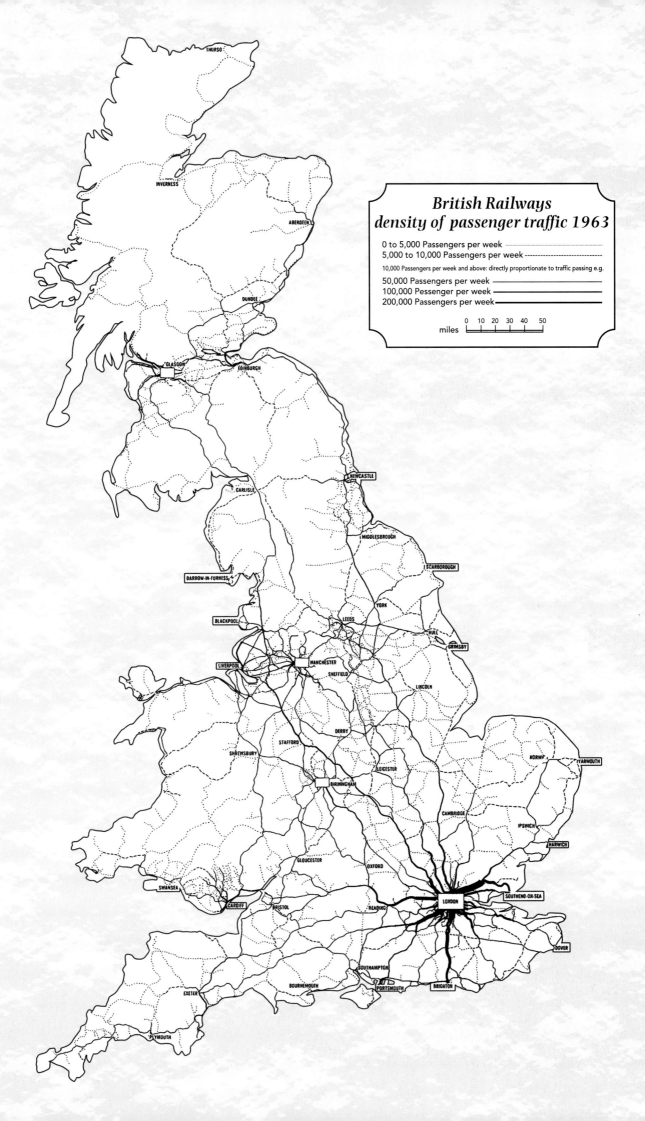

Beeching's 15-point tonic

The Reshaping of British Railways identified 15 steps which needed to be taken to bring about the turnaround in fortunes envisaged by Beeching.

These were:

1. The discontinuation of many stopping passenger services.
2. The transfer of the modern diesel multiple-unit stock displaced to continuing services which are still steam hauled.
3. The closure of a large number of small stations to passenger traffic, eliminating loss-making stops which slowed down trains.
4. Improvement to inter-city passenger services and rationalisation of routes.
5. The damping down of seasonal peaks of passenger traffics and withdrawal of corridor coaching stock held to cover them. In particular, this bode ill for branch lines serving holiday resorts, such as those on the London & South Western Railway's 'Withered Arm' system in Devon and Cornwall, where traffic levels boomed during the peak summer season but services were little used by locals during the rest of the year. The annual cost of providing the 6000 coaches for the summer season was £3.4 million, set against total revenue of just £500,000.
6. The co-ordination of suburban train and bus services and charges.
7. The co-ordination of passenger parcels service with the Post Office.
8. An increase in block train movements of coal by inducing the National Coal Board to provide train-loading facilities at collieries and the provision of coal concentration depots.
9. The reduction of uneconomic freight traffic by closing small goods stations and the adjustment of charges, in other words, the end of the traditional pick-up goods, with road hauliers ready and willing to fill the void.
10. The attraction of more sidings-to-sidings traffic by the operation of through trains at the expense of the system of forwarding of single wagons.
11. The study and development of the "liner" train system.
12. The concentration of the freight sundries traffic on 100 main depots.
13. The rapid and progressive withdrawal of freight wagons over the following three years.
14. The continued replacement of steam by diesel traction for main line services up to a probable requirement of at least 3750 to 4250 locomotives. At the time of the report, 1698 diesels were already in service and 950 on order.
15. The rationalisation of the composition and use of the railways' road cartage fleet.

'Giant Strides' is an A N Wolstenholme poster produced for British Railways to promote improvements in the speed of trains on the London-South Wales route with the introduction of diesels that travelled at 90mph. NRM

A single green railcar waits at the GWR's Bromyard station, although there were far more weeds than passengers by the time it closed on September 7, 1969. GREAT WESTERN TRUST

both forms of public transport are fighting a losing battle against private transport.

"Immediately prior to the war, in 1938, the number of private cars registered was 1,944,000. In 1954 there were 3,100,000, and in 1961 there were 6,000,000. By 1970 it is expected that there will be a total of 13,000,000 cars registered, equivalent to 24.3 per 100 of the population or 76 per 100 families."

Looking back, major flaws in the report may be seen as a failure to consider neither reduction of costs on lossmaking services and electrification to countermand competition from road alternatives. Neither were subsidies considered or asked for, as Beeching intended that his slimline railway network would eliminate its deficit within a few years.

When the report was debated by both the Commons and the country, it was in the year leading up to a general election. It might therefore seem surprising that such unpopular measures were introduced before an election rather than after it.

Yet while the Labour opposition led by Harold Wilson said it would reverse the Beeching cuts if elected, the Conservatives steamed ahead with implementation.

There appeared to be a general feeling that once protestors had been given their chance to vent their anger through initial newspaper headlines, there would be a

Railcar W51360 at Uxbridge on the last day of passenger services on the branch. GREAT WESTERN TRUST

growing general acceptance that closures were inevitable.

Marples approved the vast majority of closures which reached him for consideration, although the consultative machinery conveniently held back the first impact of the programme until the election campaign was underway.

The few he spared from the axe included important electrified commuter routes such as Manchester to Bury and Liverpool to Southport.

In February 1964, Marples made one concession – promising to close no seaside branch lines before October that year, so people could plan their holidays for the coming summer.

Passenger services on the Lostwithiel-Fowey branch were withdrawn on January 4, 1965, although the line remained in use as far as Carne Point for china clay shipping. The other rail route to Fowey, the Cornwall Minerals Railway line from St Blazey to the west, which lost its passenger services as early as September 21, 1925, was also closed in the late Sixties, but deemed so useful as a china clay freight route that after the rails were lifted, it was turned into a private road for heavy lorries. The 2.35pm Lostwithiel-Fowey branch train railcar is seen at Golant Halt on September 7, 1964. ANDREW MUCKLEY/RM

The Hayling Island branch was closed by Beeching on November 3, 1963 even though it made a small profit. British Railways gave the reason as the cost of replacing the timber swing bridge which crossed Langstone Harbour comprised an unreasonably large investment.
HUGH BALLANTYNE

Passenger services earmarked for withdrawn under Beeching report 1963

Western England
- Avonmouth Dock-Bristol Temple Meads, Filton J-St Andrews Road 11/64
- Axminster-Lyme Regis, 11/65
- Barnstaple Junction-Ilfracombe, 10/70
- Barnstaple Junction-Taunton, 10/66
- Barnstaple Junction-Torrington, 10/65
- Bath Green Park-Bournemouth West, BGP-Poole 3/66
- Bath Green Park-Bristol Temple Meads, BGP-Mangotsfield 3/66
- Bere Alston-Callington, C-Gunnislake 11/66
- Berkeley Road-Sharpness, 11/64
- Bodmin Road-Bodmin North-Wadebridge-Padstow, BN-Padstow 1/67, Halwill Jct-W 10/66, BR-Nanstallon Halt 1/67
- Bridport-Maiden Newton, 5/75
- Bristol Temple Meads-Clifton Down-Pilning, Pilning J-Severn Beach 11/64
- Bristol Temple Meads-Patchway-Pilning (local?)
- Bristol Temple Meads-Portishead, Parson Street-P 9/64
- Bude-Okehampton, 10/66
- Calne-Chippenham, 9/65
- Chard Central-Chard Junction, 9/62 (and to Creech Jct)
- Cirencester Town-Kemble, 4/64
- Clevedon-Yatton, 10/66
- Exeter Central-Exmouth –
- Exmouth-Tipton St John's, 3/67
- Fowey-Lostwithiel, 1/65
- Gloucester Central-Hereford, 11/64
- Halwill-Torrington, 3/65
- Holt Junction-Patney and Chirton, 4/66
- Kemble-Tetbury, 4/64
- Liskeard-Looe –
- Minehead-Taunton, 1/71
- Okehampton-Padstow, O-Wadebridge 10/66, W-P 1/67
- Seaton (Devon)-Seaton Junction, 3/66
- Sidmouth-Sidmouth Junction, 3/67
- St Erth-St Ives (Cornwall) –
- Staines West-West Drayton and Yiewsley, 3/65
- Taunton-Yeovil Pen Mill, T-Yeovil Town 6/64, YT-YPM 11/65
- Tiverton Junction-Tiverton, 10/64
- Yeovil Junction-Yeovil Town, 3/67

Services earmarked for closure before Beeching report
- Abingdon-Radley, 9/63
- Banbury-Princes Risborough, (local) 1/63
- Brent-Kingsbridge, 9/63
- Brixham-Churston, 5/63
- Castle Cary-Taunton, (local) 9/62
- Chalford-Gloucester, (local) 11/64
- Chard Junction-Taunton, 9/62
- Cheltenham-Kingham, 10/62
- Chipping Norton-Kingham, 12/62
- Coaley-Dursley, 9/62
- Didcot-Newbury, 9/62, excursions until 8/63
- Dulverton-Exeter St Davids, 10/63
- Gwinear Road-Helston, 11/62
- Hemyock-Tiverton Junction, 9/63
- Launceston-Plymouth, L-Tavistock Jct 12/62
- Newquay-Chacewater-Truro, N-C 2/63, C 10/64
- Oxford-Princes Risborough, 1/63
- Witham-Wells-Yatton, 9/63

Additional services listed for closure after Beeching report up to 1968
- Bath Spa-Bristol (Temple Meads) (locals only) 1/70
- Gloucester Eastgate/Central-Stratford-upon-Avon, Cheltenham Spa (Lansdown Jct)-S-u-A 3/68

Southern England
- Alton-Winchester City, 2/73
- Andover-Romsey, Andover JCT-R 9/64
- Ashford (Kent)-Hastings –
- Ashford (Kent)-New Romney, Appledore-NR 3/67
- Bexhill West-Crowhurst, 6/64
- Bournemouth-Ringwood-Brockenhurst, Broadstone-Brockenhurst 5/64
- Brighton-Horsham, Shoreham-Christ's Hospital 3/66
- Brighton-Tonbridge, Lewes-Uckfield 5/69, Groombridge-T 7/85
- Clapham Junction-Kensington Olympia –
- Eastbourne-Tonbridge, Hailsham-Eridge 6/65, Hailsham-Polegate 6/65, Groombridge-Tonbridge 7/85
- Guildford-Horsham, 6/65
- Portsmouth-Botley-Romsey/Andover, Andover Jct-R 9/64, Eastleigh-R 5/69
- Ryde Pier Head-Ventnor/Cowes, Ryde St Johns-C 2/66
- Three Bridges-Tunbridge Wells West, TB-Ashurst Jun 1/67, AJ-Groombridge 1/69

Services with intermediate stations withdrawn
- Haywards Heath-Seaford (local)
- Portsmouth-Netley-Southampton-Romsey/Andover (local)
- Reading Southern-Guildford-Redhill-Tonbridge (local)

Services earmarked for closure before Beeching report
- Havant-Hayling Island, 11/63
- Haywards Heath-Horsted Keynes, 10/63
- Selsdon-Woodside (Surrey), 5/83
- *Withdrawal already implemented

Additional services listed for closure after Beeching report up to 1968
- Eridge-Hurst Green Jct –
- Fawley-Totton (light railway) 2/66

North London
- London Broad Street-Richmond –
- Croxley Green-Watford Junction, CG-Bushey & Oxhey 6/66
- Belmont-Harrow and Wealdstone, 10/64
- St Albans Abbey-Watford Junction –
- London St Pancras-Barking (local)

Additional services listed for closure after Beeching report up to 1968
- *Uxbridge Vine Street-West Drayton and Yiewsley, 9/62
- Greenford-West Ealing –

Midlands
- Banbury/London Marylebone-Leicester Central-Nottingham Victoria-Sheffield Victoria-York, Aylesbury-Sheffield 9/66 but Rugby-Nottingham 5/69, Sheffield Victoria 1/70
- Banbury-Woodford Halse, 9/66
- Birmingham New Street-Sutton Park-Walsall, Castle Bromwich-W 1/65
- Bletchley-Buckingham, Buckingham-Verney Jct 9/64
- Bromyard-Worcester Shrub Hill, B-Henwick 9/64
- Burton-on-Trent-Leicester London Road, 9/64
- Burton-on-Trent-Wolverhampton High Level, Winchnor JCT-Walsall 1/65
- Buxton-Millers Dale, 3/67
- Derby Friar Gate-Nottingham Victoria, DFG-New Basford 9/64
- Dudley-Old Hill, 6/64
- Dudley-Walsall, 7/64
- Dunstable North-Hatfield, 4/65
- Great Bridge-Swan Village, Dudley Port-SV 6/64, Dudley-DP 7/64
- Kettering-Melton Mowbray-Nottingham Midland, local 4/66, express 4/67
- Leamington Spa Avenue-Coventry-Nuneaton Trent Valley, 1/65, LS-C reopened 5/77, C-NTV reopened 5/87
- Leicester London Road-Melton Mowbray-Peterborough North – Locals
- Newport Pagnell-Wolverton, 9/64
- Northampton Castle-Wellingborough Midland Road-Peterborough East, 5/64
- Nottingham Midland-Worksop, NM (Radford)-W 10/64, Mansfield-Radford reopened 11/95
- Peterborough East-Rugby Midland, 6/66
- Rugeley Trent Valley-Walsall, 1/65, reopened to Hednesford 4/89, to Rugeley 6/97
- Seaton-Stamford, Seaton-Luffenham 6/66 ➤

Doomed Dolgellau station on the line to Ruabon, as seen on July 1, 1967. GREAT WESTERN TRUST

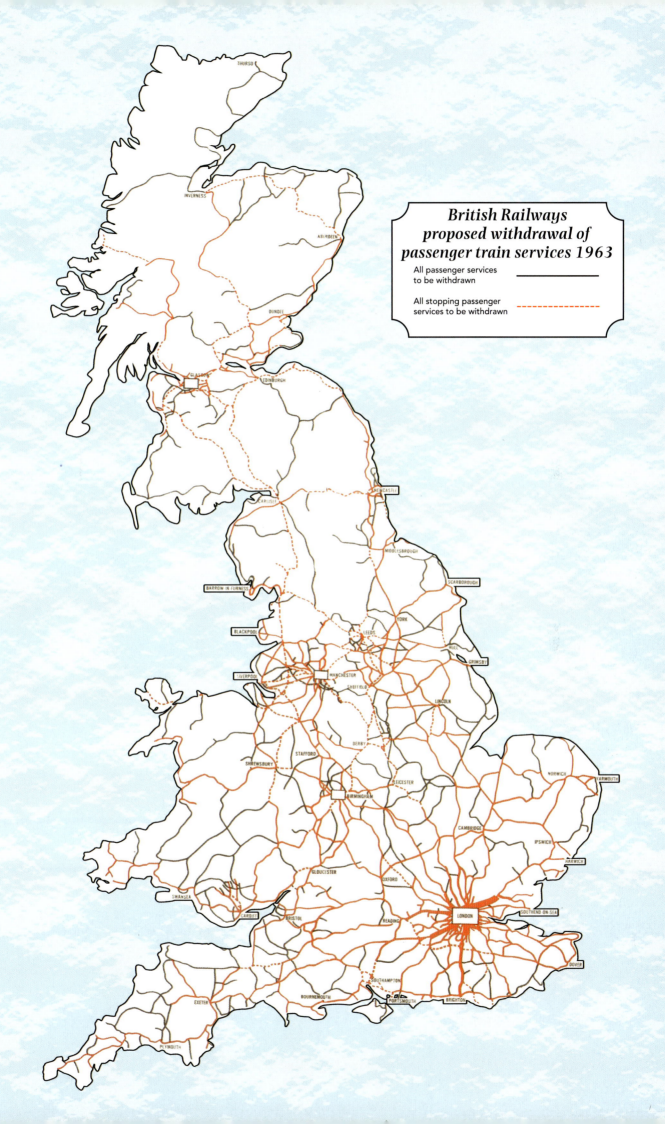

Services with intermediate stations withdrawn
- Birmingham New Street-Tamworth-Derby Midland (local)
- Derby Midland-Trent-Nottingham Midland (local)
- Derby Midland-Sheffield Midland (local)
- Derby Midland-Chinley-Manchester Central (local)
- Kettering-Leicester London Road (local)
- Leicester London Road-Nottingham Midland (local)
- Nottingham Midland-Sheffield Midland (local)

Services earmarked for closure before Beeching report
- Ashchurch-Evesham-Redditch, E-R 10/62, E-A 6/63
- Aylesbury Town-Sheffield Victoria (local), 3/63
- Hartlebury-Shrewsbury, S-Bewdley 9/63, B-H 1/70
- *Kidderminster-Tenbury Wells, TW-Bewdley 8/62
- *Kimberley East-Pinxton South, 1/63
- *Leicester Belgrave Road-Skegness, 9/62 (excursions)
- *Much Wenlock-Wellington (Salop), 7/62
- *Stourbridge Junction-Wolverhampton Low Level, 7/62

Additional services listed for closure after Beeching report up to 1968
- Ambergate South Jct-Chinley North Jct, Matlock-Chinley NJ 7/68
- Birmingham (New Street)-Redditch, Redditch (Old)-(New) 7/72
- Birmingham (New Street)-Worcester (Shrub Hill) –
- Trent (Long Eaton Jct-North Erewash Jct) 1/67
- Trent (Station North Jct-Trowell Jct)/Sawley Jun, TSNJ-TJ 11/67, TSNJ- SJ 3/67

Eastern England
- Aldeburgh-Saxmundham, 9/66
- Audley End-Bartlow, 9/64
- Barton-on-Humber-New Holland Town –
- Braintree & Bocking-Witham (Essex) –
- Brightlingsea-Wivenhoe, 6/64
- Buntingford-St Margarets, 11/64
- Cambridge-St Ives-March, C–St Ives 10/70, St Ives-M 3/67
- Dereham-Wells-Next-The-Sea, 10/64 (D-Wymondham 10/69, Kings Lynn-D 9/68)
- Firsby-Skegness – but Firsby 10/70
- Firsby-Woodhall Junction-Lincoln Central, 10/70
- Grimsby-Spalding-Peterborough North, G-Firsby 10/70, Boston-PN 10/70, S-PN reopened 6/71
- Lincoln St Marks-Nottingham Midland –
- Mablethorpe-Willoughby, 10/70
- Maldon East and Heybridge-Witham (Essex), 9/64
- Marks Tey-Shelford, Sudbury-S 3/67
- Melton Constable-Sheringham, 4/64
- Mundesley-on-Sea-North Walsham, 10/64
- Romford-Upminster –
- Swaffham-Thetford, 6/64
- Westerfield-Yarmouth South Town, Beccles-YST 11/59

Services with intermediate stations withdrawn
- Cleethorpes-New Holland Pier (local)

Services earmarked for closure before Beeching report
- Boston-Woodhall Junction, 6/63
- *Grantham-Lincoln Central, 9/62 (local), 11/65 (all)
- Immingham Dock-New Holland, Goxhill-ID 6/63
- *Palace Gates-Stratford, 1/63

Additional services listed for closure after Beeching report up to 1968
- March-Wisbech East, March-Magdalen Road 9/68

North Wales
- Afon Wen-Bangor, AW-Caernarfon 12/64, C-Menai Bridge 1/70
- Amlwch-Bangor, A-Gaerwen 12/64
- Blaenau Ffestiniog-Llandudno –
- Chester General-Holyhead/Caernarfon (local), see above

South and Mid Wales
- Abercynon-Aberdare, 3/64, reopened 10/88
- Aberystwyth-Carmarthen, A-Strata Florida 12/64 (flooding), SF-C 2/65
- Bala-Bala Junction, 1/65
- Barry-Bridgend, 6/64
- Bridgend-Treherbert, Cymmer Afan-B 6/70, CA-T 2/68 on closure of Rhondda tunnel, B-Maesteg reopened /92
- Caerphilly-Senghenydd, S-Aber J Halt 6/64
- Cardiff Clarence Road-Cardiff General, 3/64
- Cardiff-Coryton –
- Llanfyllin-Llanymynech, 1/65
- Maerdy-Porth, 6/64
- Morfa Mawddach (Barmouth Jct)-Ruabon, 1/65, but Bala-Llangollen 12/64 (flooding)
- Welshpool-Whitchurch (Salop) 1/65

Services earmarked for closure before Beeching report
- *Brecon-Hereford, 12/62
- *Brecon-Moat Lane Junction, 12/62
- *Brecon-Neath Riverside, 10/62
- *Cardiff/Barry-Pontypridd, Cadoxton-Treforest 9/62, St Fagans-Tynycaeau JUN 9/62
- *Cardigan-Whitland, 9/62
- Carmarthen-Llandilo, 9/63
- Dowlais Cae Harris-Nelson and Llancaiach, 6/64
- *Hirwaun-Merthyr, 12/62
- Pontypool Road-Aberdare High Level-Neath General-Swansea High Street, PR-NG 6/64
- Porthcawl-Pyle, 9/63
- Shrewsbury-Craven Arms-Llandovery-Pontardulais-Swansea Victoria/Llanelli, P-SV 6/64
- *Swansea High Street-Neath General-Treherbert, Briton Ferry-Cymmer Afan 12/62, CA-T 2/68

Additional services listed for closure after Beeching report up to 1968
- Whitland-Pembroke Dock –

North West
- Bacup-Bury-Manchester Victoria, Bacup-Rawtenstall 12/66, R-Bury 6/72
- Barrow-Whitehaven –
- Blackpool North-Fleetwood, F-Wyre Dock 4/66, WD-Poulton-le-Fylde 6/70
- Bury Bolton Street-Manchester Victoria, BBS-Clifton JUN 12/66
- Buxton-Manchester Piccadilly –
- Carlisle-Penrith-Workington, P-Keswick 3/72, K-W 4/66
- Carlisle-Silloth, 9/64
- Carlisle-Skipton –
- Carnforth-Wennington – but Morecambe-Wennington 1/66
- Chester General-Liverpool Lime Street –
- Colne-Accrington-Bury-Manchester Victoria, A-Ramsbottom 12/66, R-B 6/72
- Crossens-Southport Chapel Street, Preston-S 9/64
- Earby-Barnoldswick, 9/65
- Etruria-Kidsgrove (Stoke Loop), 3/64
- Glazebrook-Stockport Tiviot Dale, 11/64
- Glazebrook-Wigan Central 11/64
- Greenfield-Stalybridge-Manchester Exchange – but ME 5/69
- Hadfield/Glossop-Manchester Piccadilly –
- Hayfield/Macclesfield-Romiley-Manchester Piccadilly, H-New Mills 1/70, M-Rose Hill (Marple) 1/70
- Lake Side (Windermere)-Ulverston, 9/65 for extant excursion traffic
- Lancaster Castle/Lancaster Green Ayre-Heysham, LC-LGA 1/66, Morecambe (Torrisholme Js No1-No2) 1/66
- Leek-Uttoxeter, 1/65
- Liverpool Exchange-Fazakerley-Wigan Wallgate –
- Liverpool Exchange-Southport Chapel Street –
- Liverpool Lime Street-St Helens-Wigan North Western –
- Manchester Central-Chinley-Hope-Sheffield Midland –
- Manchester Victoria-Horwich, H-Black Rod 9/65
- Manchester Victoria-Newton Heath-Middleton, Middleton-Middleton JUN 9/64
- Moor Row-Sellafield, MR-Egremont (workmen's) 9/65
- New Brighton-Chester Northgate-Wrexham Central – Locals
- Preston-Southport Chapel Street, 9/64
- Rose Grove-Todmorden, 11/65
- Royton-Royton Junction, 4/66
- Silverdale-Stoke-on-Trent. 3/64
- St Helens Shaw Street-Earlestown-Warrington Bank Quay, StHSS-StH J 6/65
- Stafford-Wellington, 9/64

Cheltenham St James is the Regency spa town's 'lost' terminus. It was the closure of the Midland & South Western Junction Railway on September 9, 1961 followed by the GWR route on October 15, 1962 which left it being served only by trains along the line from Stratford-upon-Avon, and therefore was no longer viable. It closed to passengers on January 3, 1966 and coal traffic on October 31, 1966. GREAT WESTERN TRUST

Beeching: 55 Years of the Axe Man 51

Services with intermediate stations withdrawn
- Carlisle-Preston-Warrington-Crewe (local)
- Chester General-Crewe (local)
- Chester General-Warrington Bank Quay-Manchester Exchange (local)
- Crewe-Shrewsbury (local)
- Huddersfield-Manchester Exchange (local)
- Liverpool Lime Street-Tyldesley-Patricroft-Manchester Exchange (local)
- Manchester Exchange-Tyldesley-Wigan North Western (local)
- Oxenholme-Windermere (local)
- Shrewsbury-Wellington (local)
- Stalybridge-Stockport Edgeley (local)

Services earmarked for closure before Beeching report
- Alston-Haltwhistle, 5/76
- Cheadle (Staffs)-Cresswell (Staffs), 6/63
- Crewe-Wellington (Salop), W-Nantwich 9/63
- *Ellesmere-Wrexham Central, 9/62

Additional services listed for closure after Beeching report up to 1968
- Bamber Bridge Jct-Todd Lane Jct-Preston (East Lancashire side) 5/72
- Bootle Jct-Edge Hill, i.e. withdrawal of through services Southport (Chapel)-Euston /77
- Daisy Hill (Dobbs Brow Jct)-Blackrod (Horwich Fork JUN), 9/65
- Denton Jct-Stalybridge (via Hooley Hill) 1/68
- Denton-Droylsden 7/68
- Hadfield-Sheffield (Victoria)-Nunnery Jct: Withdrawal of electric services, Manchester (Piccadilly)-Sheffield (Victoria), remaining East Coast services to be diverted to Sheffield (Midland), H-Penistone 1/70, Penistone-Sheffield 5/83, SV 1/70
- Brindle Heath Jct-Dobbs Brow Jct-Crow Nest Jct –
- Liverpool (Exchange)-Ormskirk-Preston –
- Manchester (Victoria)-Rochdale/Oldham –
- Manchester (Victoria)-Rochdale-Todmorden –
- Preston (Todd Lane Jct-Lostock Hall Jct) 5/72
- Rochdale-Bury-Bolton-Wigan (Wallgate), R (Castleton North Jct)-Bolton (East Jct) 10/70
- St Luke's Jct-Loco Jct-Barrow Shipyard; Salthouse Jct-Loco Jct (workmen's) 7/67
- Warrington (Padgate JCT-Sankey Jct) 7/67

North East
- Bishop Auckland-Durham-Sunderland, 5/64
- Blyth-Newsham, 11/64
- Bradford Exchange-Batley-Wakefield, 9/64
- Bradford Exchange-Pudsey-Leeds Central, 6/64
- Church Fenton-Wetherby-Harrogate, 1/64
- Crook-Bishop Auckland-Darlington, C-Etherley 3/65
- Darlington-Northallerton-Harrogate-Leeds, N-H 3/67
- Darlington-Barnard Castle-Middleton-in-Teesdale, 11/64
- Darlington-Richmond, 3/69

Western Region pannier tank No. 1643 at Cardigan on the 6.50am service to Whitland on June 2, 1962. GREAT WESTERN TRUST

- Driffield-Selby, 6/65
- Goole-Selby, 6/64
- Goole-Wakefield –
- Guisborough-Middlesbrough, G-Nunthorpe 3/64
- Harrogate-Wetherby-Leeds City, W-Cross Gates 1/64
- Harrogate-York –
- Hornsea Town-Hull, 10/64
- Huddersfield-Clayton West-Penistone, CW-Shepley 1/83
- Hull-Withernsea, 10/64
- Hull-York, Beverley-Y 11/65
- Knottingley-Leeds City, Castleford Cutsyke J-Methley North J 10/68
- Leeds Central-Castleford Central-Pontefract, see above, P (Baghill)-P (Monkhill) 11/64
- Leeds City and Bradford Forster Square-Ilkley-Skipton, I-S 3/65, also Arthington-Burley-in-Wharfedale 3/65
- Malton-Whitby, M (Rillington)-Grosmont 3/65
- Middlesbrough-Whitby-Scarborough, 3/65
- Monkseaton-Blyth-Newbiggin, 11/64
- Newbiggin-Newcastle-on-Tyne, Newbiggin-Backworth, Hartley-Monkseaton 11/64
- Newcastle-on-Tyne-Washington, Pelaw-Durham 5/64
- South Shields (Tyne Dock)-Sunderland, 6/65

Services with intermediate stations withdrawn
- Bradford Exchange-Halifax-Huddersfield (local)
- Bradford Exchange-Mirfield-Huddersfield (local)
- Bradford Forster Square-Shipley-Leeds City (local)
- Doncaster-Leeds Central (local)
- Haltwhistle-Newcastle-on-Tyne (local)
- Hexham-Newcastle-on-Tyne (local)
- Leeds City and Bradford Forster Square-Keighley-Skipton (local)
- Leeds City-Cross Gates-Micklefield (local)
- Leeds City-Cudworth-Sheffield Midland (local)
- Newcastle-on-Tyne-Riverside-Tynemouth (local)
- Sunderland-West Hartlepool (local)

Services earmarked for closure before Beeching report
- Alston-Haltwhistle, 5/76
- Cheadle (Staffs)-Cresswell (Staffs), 6/63
- Crewe-Wellington (Salop), Wellington-Nantwich 9/63
- *Ellesmere-Wrexham Central, 9/62

Additional services listed for closure after Beeching report up to 1968
- Bridlington-Scarborough –
- Barnsley (Quarry Jct)-Mexborough (No 2 Box) 1/70
- Penistone (Barnsley Jct)-Barnsley (Exchange) 1/70, reopened 5/83
- Methley North Jct-Castleford (Cutsyke Jct) (Goole trains to run via Castleford Central) 10/68
- Mickle Trafford CLC Jct-Chester Northgate i.e. diversion of trains to Chester General, via Mickle Trafford LNW Jct 10/69

Scotland
- Aberdeen-Ballater, 2/66
- Aberdeen-Fraserburgh, Dyce Jct-F 10/65
- Aberdeen-Inverurie –
- Aberfeldy-Ballinluig, 5/65
- Ardrossan-Kilmarnock, Irvine-Crosshouse 4/64
- Arrochar-Craigendoran (locals) 7/64
- Aviemore-Craigellachie-Elgin, Boat of Garten-C 10/65, E-C-Keith JUN 5/68
- Ayr-Dalmellington, 4/64
- Ayr-Kilmarnock, A-Troon (Barassie) 1/67, Barassie-K 3/69
- Ayr-Stranraer –
- Ballachulish-Connel Ferry-Oban, B-CF 3/66
- Banff-Tillynaught, 7/64

- Barrhead-Glasgow St Enoch –
- Carlisle-Hawick-Edinburgh Waverley, 1/69
- Carlisle-Riddings Junction-Langholm, RJ-L 6/64
- Coatbridge-Dumbarton, Carmyle-D 10/64, Coatbridge-Rutherglen 11/66, Glasgow-Carmyle-Whifflet reopened 10/93
- Comrie-Crieff-Gleneagles, 7/64
- Darvel-Kilmanock, 4/64
- Dumfries-Castle Douglas-Kirkcudbright, CD-K 5/65, Dunragit-Dumfries 6/65
- Dumfries-Stranraer, see above
- Dunbar-Edinburgh Waverley (local?)
- Dundee-Crail-Thornton, Leuchars-St Andrews 1/69, St A-Leven 9/65, Leven-Thornton J 10/69
- East Kilbride-Glasgow St Enoch –
- Edinburgh Princes Street-Carstairs-Lanark (locals)
- Edinburgh Princes Street-Glasgow Central (via Shotts and Holytown) –
- Edinburgh Princes Street-Kingsknowe, Kinsknowe 7/64-reopened 2/71
- Edinburgh Waverley-Musselburgh, Joppa-M 9/64, Abbeyhill Jct-Piershill JUN 9/64
- Elgin-Lossiemouth, 4/64
- Fraserburgh-St Combs, 5/65
- Georgemas Junction-Thurso –
- Glasgow Buchanan Street-Stirling-Oban, Crianlarich-Dunblane 9/65
- Glasgow Queen Street-Kirkintilloch, Lenzie-K 9/64
- Glasgow St Enoch-Dalry-Kilmarnock (Lochwinnoch loop), D-Elderslie 6/66
- Glasgow St Enoch-Kilmacolm, Paisley-K 1/83
- Glasgow St Enoch-Paisley West, Paisley West 2/66
- Hamilton-Strathaven/Coalburn, 10/65
- Inverness-Kyle of Lochalsh –
- Inverness-Wick –
- Killin-Killin Junction, 9/65
- Kinross-Alloa-Stirling, K-A and locals 6/64
- Lanark-Muirkirk, 10/64
- Maud-Peterhead, 5/65
- Perth-Blair Atholl-Struan – Locals 5/65

Services with intermediate stations withdrawn
- Aberdeen-Keith-Elgin (local)
- Aviemore-Inverness-Elgin (local)
- Berwick-upon-Tweed-Edinburgh Waverley (local)
- Carlisle-Dumfries-Glasgow St Enoch (local)
- Carlisle-Glasgow Central (local)
- Fort William-Mallaig (local)
- Glasgow Buchanan Street-Stirling-Perth (local)
- Glasgow St Enoch-Lugton-Kilmarnock (local)

Services earmarked for closure before Beeching report
- *Beith Town-Lugton, 11/62
- Berwick-upon-Tweed-St Boswells, Tweedmouth-StB 6/64
- *Edinburgh Waverley-Duddingston-Morningside Road-Edinburgh Waverley, EW-D-Portobello 9/62
- *Glasgow Buchanan Street-Coatbridge Central-Holytown-Motherwell-Hamilton Central, (local) 11/62

Additional services listed for closure after Beeching report up to 1968
- Alloa (West Jct)-Larbert (Alloa Jct) 1/68
- Corstorphine-Haymarket West Jct 1/68
- Dunfermline (Touch South Jct)/Townhill Jct-Touch North Jct-Stirling (Alloa Jct), DTNJ-TJ 5/68, DTSJ-SAJ 10/68
- Grangemouth Branch Jct-Grangemouth 1/68
- Leuchars Jct-St Andrews 1/69

Thanks to Bob Lake and his http://britishrailways.info website for help in providing this information.

Main line stations axed too

Despite the national outcry over the Beeching cuts, it seemed that nobody was bothered about Flax Bourton station on the southern outskirts of Bristol. Its empty shell still stands alongside the main line to Exeter today.
MATT BUCK/
CREATIVE COMMONS

The Beeching report proposed the closure of 2363 stations and halts, of which 235 had already been closed when it was published. Indeed, in the decade following the report, around 3000 stations and halts closed, around 50% of the network total.

The closures were not always on loss-making branch lines but on retained main lines too. Poorly-patronised stations serving smaller communities were closed to passengers at first and shortly afterwards to goods, in order to eliminate the need for stopping trains and to speed up services in line for streamlining towards an inter-city network.

For example, on the West of England Main line between Bristol Temple Meads and Exeter St Davids, the route of Isambard Kingdom Brunel's Bristol & Exeter Railway, there are 22 disused railway stations, most of them closed in the 1960s. There are another 11 disused stations between Exeter St Davids and Plymouth Millbay on Brunel's South Devon Railway route.

Indeed, Ernest Marples reported that regarding Flax Bourton station on the outskirts of Bristol, he received not a single objection to the notice of closure. Its derelict shell still stands alongside the main line today.

While for the affected communities, losing their main line station was as bad as having a branch line axed, if it meant having to drive 10 miles or more to the nearest station, shorter times for main line services made them more attractive to the public.

At Hele & Bradninch station between Exeter and Cullompton, passenger services were withdrawn on October 5, 1964 but public freight facilities remained until May 17, 1965, while a siding to the Hele Paper factory was used into the 1980s.

Despite the lack of trains, much of the derelict station survives today, the empty signal box still standing at the north end of the southbound platform, the small stone booking office still on the platform next to the level crossing, and the goods shed opposite used by a garage firm.

The first stop to the south of Exeter was Exminster. It was closed to passenger traffic on March 30, 1964 and to goods on December 4, 1967, although only coal traffic had been handled for the previous 27 months. The loop sidings saw occasional use until 1985 and the signalbox was closed on November 14, 1986. The signalbox has been moved for preservation at the Gloucestershire Warwickshire Railway, but the station building very much survives in private hands as an architectural salvage depot, fenced off from the main line.

It is easy to look at the map and wonder why the station is not reopened to provide the now-sizeable community of Exminster with the ability to commute by train into Exeter, but like so many stations built by the Victorian pioneers, it stands a fair walk outside the village down a narrow country lane, and it is debatable whether residents would drive there just to ride three miles by train, or make the whole journey by car. Indeed, this scenario highlighted one of the dilemmas facing both Beeching and his successors.

Hele & Bradninch station has been closed for nearly half a century, but can still be recognised today. ROBIN JONES

Exminster station was one of many closed along the London to Penzance route in order to eliminate stops and speed up trains between major destinations. ROBIN JONES

LSWR O2 0-4-4T W17 *Seaview* bursts out of Ventnor Tunnel in to the island resort's station. The line south of Shanklin was closed in the mid-Sixties.
BRIAN MORRISON

LSWR Adams radial tank No. 30583 takes on water at Axminster, with the branch train to Lyme Regis which lost its services under the Beeching Axe on November 29, 1965.
BRIAN MORRISON

Ivatt 2-6-2T No. 41245 stands at Cheddar with the 3.28pm Witham to Yatton service on August 17, 1963. Part of the southern section of this GWR route survives as the East Somerset Railway.
HUGH BALLANTYNE

Chapter Six

The rationale & *the results*

The Beeching report highlighted the former Caledonian Railway cross-country route between Gleneagles, Crieff and Comrie as a prime example of why lines should be closed, despite claims that lossmaking branches nonetheless contribute revenue to the main lines they join.

The rural route had 10 trains a day in each direction with an element of summer holiday traffic. Services were operated by diesel railbuses on weekdays only over a distance of 15 miles, with connections made at Gleneagles with main line trains to and from Glasgow and Edinburgh.

The stations on the route were Gleneagles, Tullibardine, Muthill, Strageath Halt, Highlandman, Pittenzie Halt, Crieff and Comrie.

The report proposed that all stations except Gleneagles would be closed to passengers, in other words, the branch would be axed.

Explaining the rationale, the report said that around 340,000 passenger miles accrued to this service which accounted for 65,000 train miles a year. On average, this meant that there were only five passengers on board a train at any one time.

Earnings from the service were £1900 – just over a quarter of the train movement expenses of £7500. Station

Railbus M79973 at Gleneagles on last day of service on the Crieff branch in July 1964.
MICHAEL MENSING/
COLOUR-RAIL.COM

The 3.40pm Saturdays only York-Hull train headed by B1 4-6-0 No. 61012 at Beverley on August 14, 1965. JOHN A N EMSLIE/RM

terminal expenses brought the total of direct expenses to nearly £11,000, less than a fifth of which was covered by the earnings of the service. "When track and signalling expenses are added – £8200 – the total expenses are 10 times as great as the earnings of the service," the report said.

Beeching acknowledged that passengers using the branch service in combination with other services, such as the main line trains, contributed more than £12,000 to their earnings.

One of the biggest criticisms made about Beeching closures is that he failed to take into account such contributions, and that many branches should therefore remain open as "loss leaders". While it was hoped that passengers inconvenienced by the loss of branch lines would merely drive to the nearest main line station to catch the train, it transpired that instead they decided to drive all the way to their destination.

In the case of Gleneagles-Comrie, it was estimated that withdrawal of the service would result in the loss of £9000 of contributory revenue from the branch.

However, the overall net financial improvement expected from withdrawal of branch line services was said to be nearly £8400, or more than two-fifths of the existing level of total direct expenses attributable to the services, the report said. The line was closed on 6 July 1964.

Another cross-country route listed in detail for the chop was the 23 mile former Great Eastern Railway line from Thetford to Swaffham, where again, the earnings from the service between the two towns covered only a tenth of the total direct expenses.

While the gross revenue accruing to other services contributed by passengers using the Thetford-Swaffham service as part of their rail journey totalled around £16,000, the estimated net financial improvement in revenue which would result from the withdrawal of the branch service amounted to about £29,000, more than four-fifths of the total direct expenses. So Swaffham, the Junction for lines to King's Lynn, Dereham and Thetford via Roudham Junction, closed in 1968.

A third case study explained in detail as the North Eastern Railway's route from Hull to York via Beverley, a stopping service over a distance of 42 miles, serving a rural area between the cities of Hull and York, with some commuter traffic at each end. The stations served were Hull, Cottingham, Beverley, Kiplingcotes, Market Weighton, Londesborough, Pocklington, Stamford Bridge, Earswick and York.

It was proposed to close all intermediate stations except Cottingham and Beverley.

Nine trains ran in each direction on weekdays and mostly comprised diesel multiple units. On average, there were 57 passengers on each train.

The earnings of the service were £90,400, covering the movement expenses of £84,400. However, terminal expenses brought the total of movement and terminal expenses to £107,500, so that earnings showed a shortfall of £17,100.

It was estimated that withdrawal of the service would reduce track and signalling expenses by £43,300.

Overall, the earnings showed a shortfall of £60,400, equivalent to two-fifths of the total direct expenses of £150,800.

Because alternative services would be available after withdrawal of the service, £25,600 of the earnings would be retained.

It was estimated that passengers using the service as part of their rail journey contribute £37,700 to the revenue of other services. Because of the existence of services between Hull and York via other routes, only £4900 of this amount was expected to be lost.

The total loss in gross revenue resulting from withdrawal of the service was estimated at £69,700, but the overall net financial improvement was expected to be £81,000, equivalent to over half of the total direct expenses.

So the writing was on the wall for the route. While trains still serve Beverley and Cottingham as part of the Yorkshire Coast Line to Scarborough via Bridlington and Filey, the Beverley to York section fell victim to the Beeching Axe on 29 November 1965.

A minimalist operation using a small railbus was not enough to save Tetbury station from closure. ANDREW MUCKLEY/RM

Minimalist operations were not enough

It is often said that many Beeching closures could have been prevented if branch lines had been pared down to the bare minimum in terms of staffing levels, and operated by diesel railbuses. Indeed, looking at the number of people employed at even little-used stations back in the Fifties, from the stationmaster, signalmen booking clerks down to porters, it comes as little surprise that many rural lines did not pay.

In the late Fifties, British Railways indeed began to experiment with railbuses produced by a number of different manufacturers, such as Waggon und Maschinenbau, Park Royal and Wickham, years before Beeching arrived.

On February 2, 1959, a pair of AC Cars railbuses were introduced on the two branches that joined the Swindon-Gloucester main line at Kemble, the 4½ mile line to Cirencester Town and the 11 mile line to Tetbury.

Until then, patronage on both had been in decline. Passenger services on the Tetbury branch ran on weekdays only and consisted of six pull-push workings in each direction using auto trains. Two trains in each direction were mixed and these catered for most of the main freight traffic of coal and farm foodstuffs, as the afternoon freight train on Mondays to Fridays only ran if required. By 1958 the services had been reduced by one train and the pull-and-push sets had disappeared, while the freight levels had fallen so that only one of the two mixed trains ran as such. On the busier Cirencester branch there were nine up and 10 down trains, with two extra on Saturdays. Two of the trains each day were mixed.

With the introduction of the railbuses, services on the Cirencester branch were increased to 14 trains in each direction on Mondays to Fridays, with an extra two on Saturdays, while Sunday services remained unchanged at four in each direction. On the Tetbury branch trains were increased from five to eight on Mondays to Fridays, with an extra working on Saturdays, but the branch remained without a Sunday service.

At the same time a new halt was opened at Chesterton Lane, near Cirencester, and on the Tetbury branch halts were provided at Church's Hill and Trouble House, a pub of the same name in the middle of nowhere. Culkerton was

The Trouble House Inn, where locals set out to cause trouble for Dr Beeching. ROBIN JONES

58 Beeching: 55 Years of the Axe Man

Above: **The engine shed is all that remains of the station complex at Tetbury today, although brickwork in the adjacent public car park surface has been arranged to resemble rails.**
ROBIN JONES

reopened as an unstaffed halt, using the existing platform, but the others had ground-level platforms 25ft long and 8ft 6in wide, built of old sleepers. An additional halt at Park Leaze, between Chesterton Lane and Kemble, was opened on January 4, 1960, when running schedules were slightly amended and an extra afternoon train provided.

The four-wheeled railbuses seated 46 passengers and were fitted with automatic doors and retractable steps for use at the halts. Cheap-day facilities were available from all stations and halts, and guards were supplied with Setright ticket machines similar to those used by many bus companies. They also carried mail and parcels.

The experimental railbuses services were successful and the Cirencester branch more than 2500 passengers a week were carried in the first year. While the Tetbury branch carried only a tenth of this, the figure of 12,800 represented two-and-a-half times the annual number of passengers carried on the steam-hauled services.

Indeed, the Cirencester railbuses were often overcrowded with passengers on Saturdays.

However, despite the early positive indications, the receipts from both services did justify their retention in the eyes of British Railways.

Local pro-rail campaigners questioned the validity of the British Railways' figures, in particular those for the Cirencester branch. Despite local protests, passenger services were withdrawn from both branches from April 6, 1964.

When the Tetbury services ended on Saturday, April 4, the last down train was hampered by bales of blazing straw which had been laid across the rails.

There was trouble at Trouble House Halt, both when steam on the Tetbury branch ended, and when the line closed altogether.

When the last steam services ran on January 31, 1959, the demand for seats on the train known as the 'Tetbury Donkey' was so great that a brake van had to be added behind the 58XX 0-4-2T and its coaches. As the train neared Trouble House Halt on the return trip, someone pulled the communication cord and the passengers alighted and went to the pub for half an hour until

So typical of forgotten railways across the country: the site of the short-lived Trouble House Halt on the Tetbury branch.
ROBIN JONES

summoned back by the engine's whistle. Back at Tetbury, the passengers formed a procession headed by top-hatted mourners and marched through the town.

In 1964, a coffin covered with inscriptions, filled with empty whisky bottles and addressed to Beeching, was loaded by mourners in bowler hats at Trouble House Halt on the last advertised train to Kemble. There, it was transferred to the London train for delivery to the doctor. Incidentally, the name of the pub which stands alongside the A433 does not derive from drunken disorder or the like, but from a nearby patch of waterlogged difficult-to-farm ground known as the Troubles.

On the following day a special steam pull-and-push train, worked by Collett 14XX 0-4-2T No 1472, ran over both branches, and on the last down train on the Cirencester branch passengers were treated to free rolls and beer.

An attempt was made to burn a 6ft effigy of the Minister of Transport, but the railway police intervened and so the demonstrators set it alight on the pavement outside the terminus.

Beeching: 55 Years of the Axe Man **59**

The last cross-border passenger trains between Berwick-on-Tweed and St Boswells ran on June 13, 1964. BR standard 4MT 2-6-0 No 76050 is seen with the one-coach train from Kelso approaching St Boswells on April 11, that year. VERDUN WAKE/RM

By 1965 Beeching had reshaped that culture, and such economies might well have been possible on lines where the losses might have been reduced to acceptable levels. However, even he could not place the cart before the horse, and in any case, he had pointed out that reducing the cost of running trains by use of railbuses was not enough; the cost of providing the route itself was the key factor.

The first of the many

Ironically, among the first lines endorsed by Beeching for full closure was the Helston branch, where the Great Western Railway had pioneered the use of buses.

Local people saw closures elsewhere in the late fifties and felt that the writing was on the wall for the line.

When the end for passenger services came on November 3, 1962, it was one of the first acts carried out by the new British Railways chairman, and pre-dated his 1963 report that came out the following year. However, the work involved in the compilation of the report would have included the Helston branch, which even dieselisation could not save from becoming the first of the Cornish branch lines to close.

In scenes that would in the next few years be repeated all over the country, local residents did everything they could in a desperate bid to try to save the branch, but many of them were already using cars as the main or only form of transport. A promise to improve the road between Helston and Redruth made at the time of closure was never carried out.

The first of the 1963 report closures involved the cessation of passenger services on September 9, that year between Newcastle Central, Usworth and Washington on the Leamside line, which itself was not closed as that stage. Indeed, out of 300 service withdrawal proposals contained in the Beeching report, this was one of only two, along with Stalybridge-Biggle which did not prompt objections.

The October 1963 of the industry newspaper Railnews reported the Newcastle-Washington closure as a peaceful affair, with the headline "So Quiet, The First Beeching Closure".

The Tetbury branch was closed completely but freight lingered on the Cirencester branch until October 4, 1965.

The use of railbuses on the Dunmere Junction to Bodmin North branch in 1964 following the withdrawal of steam passenger services between Bodmin North and Wadebridge similarly proved insufficient to save the line.

Nevertheless, the railbuses had proved that rural lines could be made more attractive to the public, even if losses were not eradicated. So why did Beeching not prune more branch lines to basic one-engine-in-steam routes with unmanned stations and halts and operated by the bare minimum staff to keep them open?

The British Railways of 1961 when he took over was markedly different to the one he transformed over the following four years. Opposition to mass redundancies would have automatically come from trade unions single-mindedly protecting the rights of a multitude of very poorly-paid workers, and moves towards wholesale rationalisation would have been quickly deflected as an unacceptable culture shock.

It would not remain so for long.

Seaside lines were particularly badly hit by Beeching. Because most people who rode on them were visitors, were neither regular passengers nor even resident in the area, there were few users on hand to campaign against closure, or even to write a brief letter of objection to the Transport Users Consultative Committee.

So branches to coastal resorts had the least chance of any effective voice being raised in their support. Occasionally, hoteliers, bed-and-breakfast establishment owners and traders protested that closures would ruin their livelihood, but they were dismissed as insignificant, especially as soaring car ownership would ensure that the same number of visitors came. Actually, in the case of many traditional resorts, history records that it never did.

The background assumption that rail passengers were by now car-less minority whose numbers would diminish, whether or not Beeching's cuts went ahead, proved too strong for fragmented and localised protests.

The waiting vultures pounce

A marked feature of the Beeching era closures was the haste in which closed railways were ripped up by demolition contractors so as to realise the scrap value as quickly as possible.

Sceptics, however, had a different view, they said it was evidence of a hidden agenda to get rid of railways so that they could never be reopened again in private hands, and compete with road transport.

Railway historian TWE Roche campaigned to save the GWR South Brent to Kingsbridge branch which closed on September 14, 1963. As a result of a letter printed in *The Railway Magazine* around that time, he received a large number of letters from as far afield as Ireland, Wales and Sussex expressing interest, pledging voluntary labour and some even giving money.

He wrote to British Railways and three local councils in the hope of forming a Primrose Railway Preservation Society, with the local authorities helping to operate it as a private venture.

On October 11 that year, he wrote to the divisional manager of the Western Region at Plymouth, asking what figure the British Railways Board wanted for the branch. The divisional manager acknowledged the letter on October 17, stating he would write again when in a position to do so.

On November 4, Roche was warned by a private contact that the track was about to be lifted.

Exhaustive inquires led to confirmation on November 8 that the Civil Engineer's Department at Paddington was about to sign contracts for lifting that same day.

Roche protested, but managed to obtain only a week's stay of execution.

He wrote: "I had arranged to meet the Joint Railways Committee of the three local councils in Kingsbridge on November 25, and duly did so, an officer of the Devon County Council being present. After a very long and considerate discussion they decided they could not proceed with the scheme in view of the uncertainty about the lifting tenders and the future of Brent, although it was quite evident that, had they been assured on these matters

Left: **Blackpool Central station in July 1965, a year after it closed. The trackbeds have been infilled up to platform level and covered with Tarmacadam so it can be used as a car park, while the station buildings were converted into a bingo hall.** RM

Below: **Oswestry station, once the headquarters of the pre-Grouping Cambrian Railways, was closed to passengers on November 7, 1966, disenfranchising the town which now has a population of more than 17,000.** MIKE ESAU

One of the biggest follies of the Sixties was the continued production of first generation diesel types at the same time as the Beeching cuts were rendering them obsolete. For example the Western Region diesel hydraulic Class 14s were designed to replace steam on branch lines, and 56 were built at Swindon from 1964-5. Yet Beeching eradicated the pick-up goods they were designed, as well as many of the lines to which they were allocated. Superb machines, many of them were sold off into industrial service after less than a handful of years in British Rail service, 23 made it into preservation, including D9523 seen at Wansford on the Nene Valley Railway. ROBIN JONES

and had they had time to give the full financial facts adequate thought, the councils would have seriously considered taking over the line.

"It was fortunate they did not do so, for that very afternoon I encountered the first three of the contractors' men beginning to dismantle track in Kingsbridge station yard. Their contract, they told me, was to lift all tracks, signals, signalling equipment and steel bridges, but not granite bridges, station buildings or platforms or signal boxes. In the words of their foreman, very soon there would be nothing left at all.

"I feel that the extreme haste with which the lifting of the Kingsbridge line has been undertaken has robbed the South Hams area of the chance to retain a rail service which would have been of real social value to the local inhabitants as distinct from a purely tourist attraction."

Such scenes were repeated all over the country. Barely had protestors time to gather their thoughts after a last train before their railway was no more and there was nothing left to save apart from an empty trackbed. It seemed as if British Railways was hell bent on making sure that there was no going back.

Scrap sales in 1963 realised at least £20-million and included 4000 passenger coaches, 500 locomotives, 130,000 freight wagons, four ships and 250,000 tons of rails. In 1964, up to 100 steam locomotives were disappearing each week.

Rail closures were, of course, by no means unique to Britain, Marples and Beeching. The ascendancy of the motor transport was a global phenomenon which led at one stage or another to severe pruning of many countries' rail networks.

However, compare and contrast the situation in Britain with that of France, which also had an extensive rural network. Whereas it seemed that British Railways panicked to rip up tracks almost as soon as the last passenger left the station, across the Channel many closed rural lines were left in place for a decade or more before being ripped up.

Such a move was an insurance policy in the event that road transport might just yet not turn out as all that it was meant to be.

For me, the lifting of track and in subsequent decades, the sale of strategic closed trackbeds for building development comprised two of the greatest follies of the rail closures of the 1960s, whether Beeching's name was on them or not.

Below: **A diesel multiple unit arrives at Seaton station in Rutland with a Rugby-Peterborough service on September 16, 1965, while Ivatt 2-6-2T No. 41212 stands in the bay with a push-pull connecting train for the Stamford branch. The station, along with the lines it served, closed to passengers on June 6, 1966.** HUGH BALLANTYNE

One of the shortest Beeching closures was that of the Barnoldswick branch in West Yorkshire, which ran for just a mile and 64 chains from the main line at Earby. Watched by a small group of schoolboy linesiders, with a 'last train' message chalked on its smokebox, BR Standard 2MT 2-6-2T No. 84015 is set to leave Barnoldswick with the last train on a dull September 25, 1965. The last coal train ran on July 30, 1966. HUGH BALLANTYNE

Eradication of three trunk routes

The biggest single Beeching closure was that of the Great Central route from Nottingham to Marylebone.

The rot set in during the late 1950s when vital freight traffic began to decline, and the route was neglected in favour of rival routes, such as the Midland Main Line which it largely duplicated.

In 1958, the route was transferred from the Eastern Region to the London Midland Region, where both management and staff still had loyalties to the old London Midland & Scottish Railway empire, and not a line which was long seen as a London & North Eastern Railway competitor.

Express passenger services from London to Sheffield and Manchester were discontinued in January 1960. That left just three daily 'semi-fast' London-Nottingham trains on the route.

In March 1963, just before the report was published, local trains on many sections of the route were cancelled and many of its local stations were closed. Yet there were those who still hoped that the route could be retained and improved for parcels and goods traffic.

Beeching had other thoughts, and decided that the Great Central traffic could easily be served by other routes linking London to the north.

This decision sparked widespread controversy, especially as in February 1964, as we saw earlier, Britain signed an agreement with France for the building of a Channel Tunnel. Back in 1899, the Great Central's Marylebone extension had been built to the large Berne loading gauge in the hope that it would form a link to a Channel Tunnel, and it was ready and waiting for such use.

The 9th Earl of Lanesborough, Denis Anthony Brian Butler, had a letter expanding on this single point published in the *Daily Telegraph* on September 28, 1965. It read:

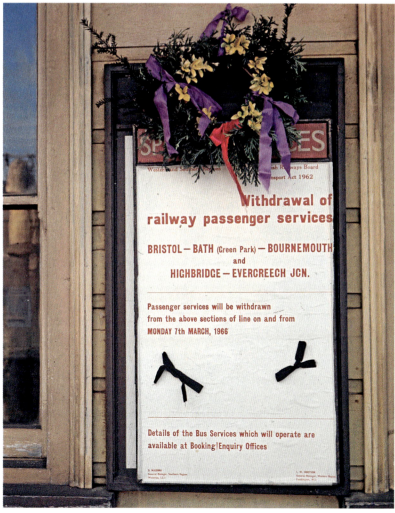

The closure notice at Evercreech Junction, the hub of the Somerset & Dorset system, on March 5, 1966. MIKE ESAU

GWR Collett 0-6-0 No 3205 heads the 2.18pm from Highbridge into Glastonbury and Street on the Somerset & Dorset 'branch' in May 1965. This locomotive survived into preservation and headed the first public train on the Severn Valley Railway in 1970. MIKE ESAU

The last day of public services on the Somerset & Dorset system was March 5, 1966, when the Locomotive Club of Great Britain ran a special from Waterloo via Bournemouth. The northbound train hauled by Bulleid Pacifics No. 34006 *Bude* **and No. 34057** *Biggin Hill* **is seen making a photographic stop at Chilcompton.** MIKE ESAU

"...surely the prize for idiotic policy must go to the destruction of the until recently most profitable railway per ton of freight and per passenger carried in the whole British Railways system, as shown by their own operating statistics.

"These figures were presented to monthly management meetings until the 1950s, when they were suppressed as "unnecessary", but one suspects really "inconvenient" for those proposing Beeching type policies of unnecessarily severe contraction of services…

"This railway is of course the Great Central forming a direct continental loading gauge route from Sheffield and the North to the Thames valley and London for Dover and France."

The sections between Rugby and Aylesbury and between Nottingham and Sheffield were closed in 1966 and the track lifted, leaving the section between Rugby and Nottingham over which diesel multiple units operated a skeleton shuttle service.

Nottingham Victoria station was closed in 1967, British Rail selling the lucrative city centre site for shopping redevelopment. As a result, trains from Rugby terminated instead at Arkwright Street station, which, ironically, had been closed in 1963. One platform was reopened to serve the six daily trains that remained.

The last train departed from Arkwright Street on Saturday, May 3, 1969. The station and viaducts carrying the railway were demolished around 1975 and the site is now occupied by housing development.

Calls to save the Somerset & Dorset Joint Railway system also fell on deaf ears.

While its Bath to Bournemouth West main line was famous as the route of the 'Pines Express' from Manchester, its stopping trains were slow. In 1938, they were recorded as taking four hours to travel from Bath to Bournemouth. Meanwhile, the S&D's original main line from Evercreech to Burnham-on-Sea, relegated to branch status when the main line to Bath opened, took 70 minutes to cover just 24 miles.

The S&D main line crossed the Southern Railway's Waterloo-Salisbury-Exeter line at Templecombe, but connections between the two were poor, and if you lived along the S&D, it was far from an ideal way by which to travel onwards to London.

Like many rural routes listed for closure by Beeching, summer Saturdays saw a huge upsurge in traffic, with 13 long-distance trains using the line, 12 to Bournemouth and the other to Exmouth and Sidmouth, via Templecombe. Running non-stop over the Mendips, they took two-and-a-half hours to run from Bath to Bournemouth.

The rundown of the S&D system began in 1951 with the withdrawal of passenger services over the short length between Highbridge and Burnham-on-Sea and the closure of the branch from Glastonbury to Wells. In December 1952, passenger services were withdrawn between Edington Junction and Bridgwater, the branch closing altogether on October 1, 1954. Four of the smaller stations in Dorset were axed as an economy measure in 1956.

The watershed came when the line north of Templecombe was transferred from the Southern Region to the Western Region in 1958. Over the next five years, through trains from the north and the Midlands including the 'Pines Express' were diverted to other routes.

A champion of the railways prepared to take on Beeching was future poet laureate John Betjeman, famous

An unidentified Modified Hall at Devizes on the 4.07pm service from Reading to Trowbridge on June 1, 1963. Devizes station and the Devizes branch line was closed in 1966 under the Beeching Axe. While the population of the town appeared to be stagnant at the time, it has since grown to 14,000, but with the trackbed sold off, reinstatement would be a costly affair.
GREAT WESTERN TRUST

Linesiders scramble to photograph 'Black Five' No. 44872 at Brackley on the last day of through working on the Great Central line.
K FAIREY/
COLOUR.RAIL.COM

Beeching: 55 Years of the Axe Man **65**

The end of the Great Central: the last train departs from Arkwright Street station on May 3, 1969.
DAVID HILLAS/CREATIVE COMMONS

Ivatt 2MT 2-6-2T No. 41243 is about to depart from Bath Green Park on April 21, 1956 with the 12.23pm local service to Bristol Temple Meads. BRIAN MORRISON

Seen at Galashiels station, Gresley A4 Pacific No. 60031 *Golden Plover* heads a Stephenson Locomotive Society special over the Waverley Route on April 16, 1965. This photograph is taken from *Last Years of the Waverley Route* by David Cross, published by Ian Allan in hardback in 2010. DEREK CROSS

for his writing about Metroland. Betjeman had been a leading figure in the battle to save the aforementioned Doric Arch at Euston, but is credited with helping to save the façade of St Pancras station, where a statue of him now stands at the new international terminus.

In summer 1962, Betjeman made *Branch Line Railway*, a BBC TV documentary on the S&D, riding on the branch from Evercreech Junction to Highbridge, asking, in vain as it turned out, Beeching to spare it from the axe.

When Labour came to power in 1964, winning two general elections, the new Government promised to end railway closures. Nonetheless, Bournemouth West was closed in 1965, S&D trains being diverted into Bournemouth Central, and the vociferous campaign to save the line was lost when in 1965 when Transport Secretary Barbara Castle confirmed the closure as outlined in the Beeching report.

The closure was set for January 3, 1966, but had to be postponed when one of the road operators withdrew his application for a licence to provide alternative road services.

An emergency four-trains-a-day service was introduced between Bath and Bournemouth, which lasted until the axe finally fell on both the main line and branch line apart from three small isolated sections kept open for freight for a few more years.

Beeching described the Waverley Route between Carlisle and Edinburgh as "the biggest money loser in the British railway system". Already, both passenger and goods traffic was being lost to road, with passenger services on its branches being progressively withdrawn. The demise had its roots in the 1930s, during the Depression which hit freight loadings from Hawick and Galashiels.

By 1954, 80% of livestock from farms, traditionally carried by rail to market, had been switched to road, and by 1963, this traffic had vanished from the route. Road transport also took over the local woollen and tweed business. In the sixties, the line had become more of a route for express rather than local freight.

Passenger services from Galashiels to Selkirk had been withdrawn on September 8, 1951, followed by Riccarton to Hexham on October 15, 1956 and the Kelso and Tweedmouth service on June 13, 1964. After the Kelso line closed to passengers, only the Carlisle to Edinburgh service remained.

Under Beeching's calculations, once the remaining freight trains and the two remaining St Pancras to Edinburgh services were rerouted on to alternative routes, only local passenger trains would be left, and along a route the southern half of which was extremely sparsely populated, the economics of the route would never stack up.

In October 1966 British Railways posted closure notices at all stations on the line with the intention of withdrawing services from January 2, 1967.

Following early protests, a brief reprieve was given when the closure was postponed pending review. Nonetheless, on July 15, 1968, the Labour Minister for Transport, Richard Marsh, announced that the line would close on January 6, 1969.

The secretary of State for Scotland was among those who protested, including local MP David Steel, the future Liberal Democrat leader. Local people collected a petition and a delegation went to London in December 1968. However, as happened so often with

Beeching closures, the views of local people were ignored. Marsh was persuaded by British Railways that the losses were too great.

The closure weekend provoked some of the most vociferous anti-Beeching protests, with banner-waving demonstrators at most stations. On January 4, British Rail ran a 'Farewell to the Waverley Route' special, while another was charted by the Border Union Railway Society, The society special, hauled by the now-preserved Deltic diesel D9002 *The King's Own Yorkshire Light Infantry*, carried a coffin bearing the inscription "Waverley Line – born 1849, killed 1969.'

The last passenger service on the line, which was also the final train to run over the entire route, was the 9.56pm Edinburgh to St Pancras sleeper on Sunday, January 5, 1969 hauled by Class 45 diesel D60 *Lytham St Annes*. At Hawick, someone tampered with a set of points to delay the already-late train and a Clayton diesel, D8506, was sent in front of the express to 'prove' the route southwards.

At Newcastleton, the train was delayed again because the level crossing gates had been padlocked with more than 200 protestors led by local vicar the Reverend Brydon Mabon standing on the line holding placards with slogans like "Stop the Great Train Robbery", "No Trains No jobs" and "Don't Cut Our Lifeline". The minister was among several arrests made – he was released only after the intervention of train passenger David Steel – and by the time the express reached Carlisle, it was two hours late.

The section from Newtongrange remained open for goods traffic as far as Hawick until April 28, 1969, the stretch from Lady Victoria colliery to Newtongrange lasting until December 20, 1971, the last traffic having been switched to road. The final section, Newtongrange to Millerhill, closed on June 28, 1972.

In 1969, a consortium calling itself the Border Union Railway Company was formed under the guidance of TV presenter Bob Symes with the aim of buying the entire route and running trains using imported German Pacifics steam locomotives. That November, British Rail demanded a deposit of £250,000, and when the company asked for extra time, the reply was that four months would be given, but interest of £8000 a month would have to be paid.

Negotiations ended two days before Christmas. It seemed that British Rail had been placing every possible obstacle in the way of the revivalists, and many thought that the powers that were simply did not want a private operator running a main line. Most of the track was lifted by early 1972.

Bizarrely, after the track had been torn up, the parcels office at Hawick stayed open so that British Rail vans continued to carry parcels traffic by road.

A delegation of Waverley Route protestors in London in December 1968, with David Steel MP in the centre. This picture has been used as part of a display outlining railway history in the Great Hall at the National Railway Museum in York. NRM

Left: **The statue of rail campaigner Sir John Betjeman at St Pancras International.** TROKA/LCR

Beeching: 55 Years of the Axe Man **67**

Class 47 diesel D1823 hauls a Freightliner train through Oxenholme on August 5, 1967.
COLOUR-RAIL.COM

Success stories:
Merry-Go-Round and Freightliner

One of the big plus points of the Beeching report as far as the improvement in rail freight services was the introduction of cost effective 'Merry-Go-Round' coal trains and Freightliner liner services.

A train of MGR wagons is able to load and unload its cargo while still moving – thereby maximising efficiency of the wagon fleet.

When 'Merry-Go-Round' services were first introduced, British Rail designed an all-new wagon with air brakes and the capacity to carry 33 tons of pulverised coal.

The prototype was a 32-ton unit, built at Darlington and tested in 1964.

West Burton power station was used as a testbed for the MGR system. However, the first power station to receive its coal by MGR wagons was Cockenzie in Scotland in 1966. It was said at the time that the 80 MGR hoppers needed to supply Cockenzie would replace up to 1500 conventional coal trucks.

With investment from the Central Electricity Generating Board and the National Coal Board, new power stations were built at Aberthaw, Drax, Didcot, Eggborough, Fiddlers Ferry and Ratcliffe to handle MGR traffic, while several existing power stations were converted to MGR operation.

After the closure of Darlington Works in 1966, Merry-Go-Round wagon production continued at Shildon – and, with the exception of 160 wagons built at Ashford – all 10,702 HAA wagons and 460 HDA wagons were built in the town.

The last 'Merry-Go-Round' wagon to be built at Shildon Wagon Works was HDA No. 368459 in 1982. Along with the prototype wagon, it is to be displayed in the Collection Building at Locomotion: the National Railway Museum at Shildon.

The Freightliner concept involves the use of reusable intermodal or shipping containers (commonly known as ISO containers) for moving products and raw materials between locations or countries. As part of Beeching's rationalisation drive, British Railways introduced a system whereby ISO containers were carried on flat wagons between a series of dedicated inland terminals, using gantry cranes for transhipment between road and rail.

Beeching originally intended Freightliner to handle domestic goods traffic, but this volume was soon surpassed by freight between deep-sea ports, such as Southampton Maritime and inland distribution terminals like Dudley, opened on the site of the town's closed station in 1967, and which became one of the most profitable in the country.

In 1995, Freightliner was privatised as a stand-alone company when it was bought out by its own management.

'Merry-go-Round' coal trains were one of Beeching's big success stories and are still very much with us today. This example is seen at Heck Ings in Yorkshire with Drax power station in the background.
BRIAN SHARPE

The Beatles meet one of their youngest fans on arrival at Minehead station. R KINGSLEY TAYLOR/MIKE CHILCOTT COLLECTION

Beeching and the Beatles

It has been said that years after he left the railways to return to ICI, the Beatles considered bringing in Dr Beeching to handle the finances of their Apple Corps company.

It did not happen, but the Beatles had already established a link of sorts with the axeman, for scenes from their first film *A Hard Day's Night* was filmed on the Minehead branch, one of the many lines earmarked for closure, in March 1964.

Hundreds of screaming schoolchildren packed platforms at stations after teachers gave time off for them to see Beatles shooting scenes for the movie.

On March 2, a special five-coach train brought the Fab Four, who had already reached No 1 in the UK charts by then, along with fellow stars Wilfred Brambell (Albert Steptoe), John Junkin, Norman Rossington and Richard Vernon and director Dick Lester from Paddington to Somerset.

The route of the train was meant to have been kept a secret, yet it soon leaked out – and with a vengeance. Newspaper headlines covering the visit and the reaction of crowds included '500 girls in Beatle battle'. The visit made the BBC national news.

In July the film opened to great critical and commercial success

Ironically, the Beatles split up around the same time that the Minehead branch line closed to passengers in early 1971. Paul McCartney went to form a band called Wings, while the other three had solo careers, and in 1976 the branch was reborn as the West Somerset Railway. It still features Western Region diesel hydraulics and British Railways Mk1 coaches, much the same as at the time of the Beatles' visit.

Other local connections are that George Harrison's wife Patti Boyd came from nearby Wellington, and animal lover Paul McCartney owns woodland near Dulverton, which stands as an obstacle in the heart of Exmoor deer hunting country.

The Beatles with Wilfred Brambell on board their train on the Minehead branch in 1964. The diesel that pulled it, Western Region diesel hydraulic Class 35 Hymek D7076, is now preserved on the East Lancashire Railway. R KINGSLEY TAYLOR/MIKE CHILCOTT COLLECTION

Chapter Seven

The backlash & *backpedalling*

Back in 1935, when a protest meeting was held in a bid to stop the Southern Railway from closing the Lynton & Barnstaple Railway, a telling question killed the debate, like a pin bursting a balloon. The packed room was asked how many attendees had travelled by the railway that day. The lack of raised hands spoke volumes.

Many railway lines that closed in the 1950s died a death with hardly a murmur. Others were marked by special enthusiasts' trains to mark the last day.

When there were local opposition groups, it was too often a case of people who might have used the railway protesting too much about the fact it would soon no longer be an option. Joni Mitchell said "you don't know what you've got til it's gone" and in so many cases that applied to branch lines. In many cases, people saw the closure notices as foregone conclusions.

However, the sheer scale of the Beeching cuts, coming on top of 780 miles closed in 1962 and another 324 in 1964, led to nationwide rather than localised anger, from rail users, local residents, civic representatives and the unions.

Protest marches were held, councils voted against closure, MPs were lobbied, accounts were disseminated to provide fresh arguments that certain lines could be made viable, but in most cases to no avail. In fairness, not every proposed closure or withdrawal of service listed in Beeching's 1963 report was carried through, but there were many other cases where local people felt that they had done enough in presenting counter arguments, only to be left with the feeling that they fell on deaf ears and had been left standing in the path of an unstoppable steamroller left on autopilot.

A rare internal view of one of the Transport Users Consultative Committee line closure enquiries, as pictures inside TUCC hearings were generally banned by the Ministry of Transport. This one took place in Huddersfield. ALAN EARNSHAW COLLECTION

A Class 101 DMU at Wells-next-the-Sea on October 3, 1964, the last day of passenger services. COLOUR-RAIL.COM

Lord Stonham, the Labour peer who had been the only member of the party ever to be elected MP for Taunton, and later won the inner London seat of Shoreditch and Finsbury, launched a broadside against the Beeching report and its backers in a speech to the House of Lords on May 2, 1963.

Beginning by mentioning the minister of transport's statement that 25,726 jobs would disappear, he said: "… the whole difficulty, the whole acute public anxiety which undoubtedly exists throughout the country about the Beeching Plan is, in my view, attributable to what the noble Viscount (Lord Hailsham) called Mr Marples' flair for publicity: the terrific public relations job which has been done on the presentation of this plan, and its blowing up out of all reasonable sense of proportion."

Commenting on Ernest Marples' statement to the Commons that the period ending in September 1964 "… will see the most intensive implementation of the plan on the assumption that closures will go as fast as anyone could reasonably expect." Lord Stonham said: "The precise mention of the number of jobs which are going to be lost indicates that the decision, in so far as it can be made, has already been made; and almost every word that the minister of transport says on this subject is proof positive that the minds of the Government have been made up."

He raised the issue of the planned closure of rail connections to Stranraer, the ferry port for Northern Ireland, asking Lord Hailsham if he was "aware that 40% of the people who go on the boat to Larne in Northern Ireland go by rail to Stranraer; that the steamer's income increased to £286,000 this year from £200,000 the year before, and that Ayrshire County Council are afraid that if the rail link is broken they will eventually lose the steamer and the short sea route to Ireland altogether?"

He described Marples' promised consultation on the Stranraer line as "the kind of consultation that a condemned man gets when they ask him what he wants for breakfast before they hang him".

Beeching: 55 Years of the Axe Man **71**

On the Isle of Wight, Beeching wanted to close everything apart from the Ryde Pier section, which would take ferry passengers from one end of the pier to the other. Local campaigners forced a compromise with Ryde-Shanklin remaining open. Why the entire line could not have been saved through to Ventnor remains a permanent subject for debate.

Steam trains were withdrawn from Ryde Pier on September 17, and the whole line on December 31, 1966, after which it was converted to allow 750V third-rail electrification to take place. At the same time, it was decided to increase the height of the trackbed in Esplanade Tunnel, to reduce flooding by very high tides and the need to pump out seawater afterwards.

The diminished clearance would no longer allow trains built to the national loading gauge to run beneath it, so rolling stock built to a lower height was required. Second-hand London Underground tube trains provided the answer and are still running there today.
SOUTH WEST TRAINS

Lord Stonham said: "Many of the figures in the Beeching Report are known to be wrong, although unfortunately none of them can be really checked."

He said that many of its provisions – the reduction in stopping and branch line services; closure of little-used wayside stations or their conversion to halts; reductions in passenger stock and wagons; great reduction in the number of marshalling yards, plus resiting and modernising; larger wagons, particularly for mineral traffic; complete reorientation of freight services to speed movement and reduce costs and provide direct transits for main streams of traffic and attract to the railway a due proportion of the full load merchandise traffic which would otherwise pass by road – had been spelled out in the British Railways 1955 Modernisation Plan. This was 'faithfully copied' into the Beeching report – despite Marples' statement that there has been nothing like it before in the history of British Railways.

He said that unlike the Modernisation Plan eight years earlier, it had "occasioned anger – anger cutting across party barriers; anger deeper and more widespread, in my opinion, throughout the country than almost any domestic issue during the last 20 years".

He asked why the only pleasant comment he had heard on the plan "is the advice to use Dr Beeching's face cream because it removes all lines".

He suggested that while the 1955 plan had been announced as being "not designed merely to make our railway system self-supporting: it aims at producing far-reaching benefits for the economy of the country as a whole and for the better ordering of its transport arrangements".

Beeching was not allowed to spare a thought for the economy of the country as a whole.

Also, whereas the Modernisation Plan aimed to benefit the whole country, including the parts furthest away from the main industrial centres like Scotland, Wales and the west of England, all of those areas would "have virtually ceased to exist" under the Beeching proposals.

Lord Stonham added: "In 1955 the same ideas were presented with wisdom as a means of rehabilitation, re-equipment and, in some cases, expansion. In 1963 it has been brutal surgery allied to mishandling so foolish as to appear deliberate."

Crucially, he shifted the blame from the man whose name appeared on the report, and which has become synonymous with rail closures. He continued: "For this I blame the Government; certainly not Dr Beeching, Indeed, one can only blame such an outstanding technologist for having accepted his task with such limited terms of reference and thus inevitably producing an intellectual exercise in a vacuum; as any plan for the railways must be when it is conducted in isolation from other forms of transport and from the economic and social needs of the country."

A penny a week 'would stave off closures'

Lord Stonham called, in vain as it turned out, for a postponement on closures until it was known what they would cost the country, and the longer-term, fundamental question of the national cost relationship between road and rail was answered. He pointed out that in recent years, 340 branch lines and 4000 miles of track had been closed – saving the railways less than 1% – or two old pence in the pound – of their total costs.

He said that the expected saving of £18 million a year by closing 5000 miles of passenger services was equivalent to just four days' defence expenditure. "Compare £18 million with the £2350 million allowed on tax-free expenses – most of it on tax-free cars," he said. "Would an £180 million branch line subsidy be a worse way of spending money than the much larger business car subsidy?

"This sum of £18 million a year means one penny a week for each one of us."

He also drew attention to the high summer patronage of closure-earmarked branch lines, when some of the doomed stations received 100 times their daily winter average of passengers, and predicted that the already-choked roads would have to shoulder this burden during holiday times if the closures went ahead.

He also questioned Marples' statement that if the railways attracted all the traffic they want from the roads after the implementation of the Beeching report, road traffic would fall by 2%. While the Beeching report proposed to cut 900 freight depots down to 100 larger ones, extra lorries would be needed, and they would all be in congested areas.

Lord Stonham criticised the minister for not having plans in place to widen and improve roads to handle the extra traffic before closing branch lines.

He said: "The closure of the marginal Peterborough-Grimsby line will isolate a large part of Lincolnshire, including towns like Skegness, which will be 23 miles from the nearest railway station. The roads are comparatively narrow and wind extraordinarily, and 150 miles will need straightening and widening. At £100,000 a mile, that means £15 million for only one area.

"In addition, it will put an enormous burden on ratepayers at the very time when they are losing income because people will not be going to the seaside resorts. How much it is going to cost on immediate works the minister does not know. My guess is that it well may be £1000 million, and as the estimates come in, that may well prove to be an underestimate. This cost alone is going to knock the £18 million a year silly. How can the closure procedure be started before this information is available?

"There are literally scores of what I regard as utterly daft proposals in this plan. In the Rhondda, there is a two-mile railway tunnel under the mountains. It is proposed to continue the railway for freight but not for passengers. To get to the other side of the mountain by road entails travelling 40 miles and the roads round are not suitable for buses.

"Out of 195,000 miles of highways, there will be thousands of miles which will need major and costly improvements if they are to carry buses and lorries safely."

Lord Stonham described as "utter nonsense" the Commons statement by Marples that 100 extra buses would cover the 15,000 square miles of Scotland left entirely without railways.

LNER V2 2-6-2 No. 60836 stands inside the impressive North Eastern Railway terminus at Alnwick waiting to work the 5.55pm to Alnmouth on June 1, 1966. The station was closed in 1968, but the trainshed remains intact and in use as a bookshop for Barter Books. The Aln Valley Railway is planning to rebuild as much of this three-mile line as possible. HUGH BALLANTYNE

Great Northern Railway-built eight-road Colwick shed (38A) at Nottingham closed on Sunday, April 4, 1965. The locality had acquired a sense of dereliction and despair by August 1971. MIKE ESAU

"What sort of confidence does it inspire when he tells the doomed areas not to worry because he personally will have to approve every closure?" he said. "That is precisely what does worry them."

In the days before Lord Stonham's speech, a resolution passed by the National Council on Inland Transport at a conference which included representatives of 170 local authorities from all parts of Britain passed a resolution which stated that it was "appalled by the social and economic consequences of Dr Beeching's Report and demands that it shall not be implemented until all the consequences and costs to the nation have been fully assessed."

The country in uproar

The County Councils Association of England and every major authority in Scotland, Wales and the west of England followed up the resolution with similar demands.

Lord Stonham said: "This adds up to a unanimous and overwhelming demand from non-party organisations representing virtually the entire population. Any minister, in my view, would have to be either mentally subnormal or morally delinquent to ignore this overwhelming demand and the local knowledge and facts on which it is based."

Regarding public subsidies to railways, Lord Stonham accused the Government of merely switching them to roads, so haulage "can profitably quote freight rates which put the railways out of business. That is the economics of Bedlam."

He said that taking into account road construction and maintenance which was rising to £250 million a year, the £230 million annual cost of accidents, £130 million spent on police signals and traffic control, the Road Federation's estimated cost of congestion placed at £500 million a year and damage to buildings at £100 million a year gave a total of £1210 million a year. With fuel duties and vehicle taxes brought in around half this sum, it revealed a net subsidy to road transport of over £600 million a year – four times the railway deficit.

"In other words, the roads are a far bigger national loss maker that the railways," he added.

Nonetheless, Lord Stonham said that he still saw "much to commend" in the Beeching report, particularly with the proposals to boost freight. "But they cannot succeed unless we see to it that they get the chance to compete (with road haulage) on equal terms," he said.

"We should ask Dr Beeching to look again, not at how easily he can close lines down, but at what must be done to keep them open.

"Give them a facelift: apply with goodwill the many methods whereby costs can be lowered by running modified services, rather than destroy them altogether.

"Use and foster the growing interest of many local authorities in their railway and their anxiety to increase its business.

"Jettison the idea, which our people will never accept, that they must holiday abroad because British Railways will make no provision for holidays in Britain.

Below: **Marching against the Beeching cuts in Manchester on October 13, 1963, a photograph displayed in the National Railway Museum's Great Hall.** NRM

Right: **Leeds Holbeck (55A)-allocated Royal Scot 4-6-0 No. 46117** *Welsh Guardsman* **awaits departure from Glasgow St Enoch on June 29, 1957 with the 'Starlight Special' for Marylebone. The station was closed on June 27, 1966 as part of the Beeching rationalisation of the local railway system, and its 250 trains and 23,000 passengers a day were diverted to Glasgow Central. The roofs of the structure and the St Enoch Hotel which fronted the station were demolished, despite protests, in 1977.** BRIAN MORRISON

"Before the war, students used to come from all over the world to watch and learn from British Railways. They will begin to come again if we call a truce to amputation, and, by infusing modern efficiency with the old spirit of public service, restore our railways to their former position as the envy of the world."

While several of the lines he mentioned were eventually spared the axe, and Skegness for one is still served by rail, most of his counter arguments against the Beeching closures fell on deaf ears.

History was left to judge how many of them were valid, balanced by the fact that despite Marples' personal interest in roads, the switch from rail to road and the growth in car ownership at the expense of railway branch lines was a global phenomenon by no means restricted to Britain.

By the time Labour replaced the Tories in office in late 1964, 'Beeching Must Go' was almost a national war cry.

To add balance to Lord Stonham's criticisms of the Beeching report, it should be remembered that while it was a Conservative government that called for the network to be rationalised, it was to be the ensuing Labour government, a party long associated with verbal support for public transport, and which before it won the general elections in 1964 pledged to reverse the Beeching cuts, that nonetheless implemented most of it. Lord Stonham went on to serve as a Home Office junior minister from 1964-67 in Harold Wilson's Labour government and as minister of state in the Home Office with responsibility for Northern Ireland until 1969, when he was appointed as a privy counsellor.

An expert's view

The Great Central Association, a corporate member of the National Council on Inland Transport, published a report by Professor E R Hondelink, MSc, MICE, MInstT, which argued that had Britain's roads been subjected to a Beeching-style study, the case for closing railways en masse would have quickly fallen through.

Prof Hondelink, a consultant to the United Nations Technical Assistance Service, said: "Dr Beeching's pronouncement that there is no sensible alternative to his plan must be challenged with the greatest vigour."

He said that the one-sided Government approach had ignored "the identical but more complicated and more serious problem of overall economic road transport deficits" and outlined the position as he saw it as follows:

"Roads provided, owned, maintained, administered and paid for by 1288 highway authorities, used by millions of transporters, individuals, groups and companies. Accounts legion in numbers, complicated and not easily analysed. Widespread research in other lands compared with position here point to the likelihood that overall deficit – ultimately born by taxpayer and ratepayer – is far in excess of the railway deficit. It is certainly at least £300 million, may well be as high as £600 million.

"If a similar exercise were carried out on the roads and road transport sector, it is probable that the bottom would fall out of Dr Beeching's report."

The professor, who had just stood down as director general of the European Central Inland Transport Organisation, and who clearly "knew his stuff", said that many rail routes had been subjected to "calculated neglect and starvation" prior to closure, and that the additional burden on the highway authorities of transferring rail traffic to roads had been ignored.

As did many critics of Beeching, he stressed the importance of loss-making branch lines as feeders of traffic to the main line, and said other countries that had closed unremunerative branch lines had later reopened them.

He urged, largely in vain at it happened, the Government to order the British Railways Board to probe road and other transport costs in the same way Beeching had addressed the railways, to postpone all closures until such studies had been completed and to immediately concentrate on making maximum and more economic use of existing equipment, while reducing staff by operational and administrative methods already in widespread use on continental Europe.

Labour's broken promise

Under Harold Wilson's Labour government elected in 1964, the pre-election promise to halt the Beeching closures was not only quickly and conveniently forgotten, but also the closures continued at a faster rate than under Marples.

In 1964, the first year that many of the Beeching recommendations took effect, 1058 miles were closed, followed by 600 in 1965, in the first year of the Wilson administration.

In December 1965, *The Railway Magazine* correspondent Onlooker, in pleading for a square deal for the railways after what he called a "year of frustration", commented: "The Reshaping report listed 267 passenger services to be withdrawn and 2363 stations and halts to be closed. Over 300 parliamentary constituencies were affected, yet not a single Tory MP voted against its approval.

"Also, since changing sides in the House, not a single Labour MP has had the courage to remind the party's leaders about this unredeemed pledge.

"Back in their constituencies, however, they bay to a different moon. Whenever a public inquiry is held by the Transport Users' Consultative Committee into a proposed withdrawal of a service, local MPs, whether Tory or Labour, line up to lead the objectors. As Hamlet might have said: 'Thus a three-line whip does make cowards of us all... and enterprises of great pith and moment, with this regard, their currents turn away and lose the name of action.'

"The root cause of Labour's betrayal of rail is not far to seek. There are 2,500,000 workers employed in the road transport industry, while the BR payroll barely reaches 500,000 – a ratio of 5 to 1. Can a government deal fairly with a plaintiff's case when there are five bellicose defendants breathing down its neck?"

In 1966, another 750 miles were closed, followed by 300 miles in 1967, 400 in 1968, 250 in 1969 and 275 in 1970. Only then did the rate of closures rapidly fall off.

So while it is easy to shift the blame for the axe on Ernest Marples, the road building minister who appointed Beeching and rubber stamped many of the closures he recommended, it was the Labour opposition that despite its public vows to reverse the trend, stuck to much the same policy once elected, when it also found that it had to make the same hard decisions based on available criteria in the face of the soaring British Railways deficit which accompanied the growth in car ownership.

'Black Five' 4-6-0 No. 45113 at Northampton Castle on May 2, 1964, the last day of services, after which the route to Peterborough closed to passengers.
K FAIREY/COLOUR-RAIL.COM

With the famous abbey on the right of the horizon, the 12.50pm Middlesbrough-Scarborough diesel multiple unit service enters Whitby on March 6, 1965, the last day of passenger services between there and Scarborough. Harold Wilson forgot his pre-election pledge to specifically save this route. MAURICE BURNS/RM

A seaside resort hit particularly hard was Whitby, where the closure of all three routes to the town was recommended. Local people widely expected the main route to York to be saved; however, in September 1964, just a month before the general election, Marples surprised everybody by confirming the closure of both the York and Scarborough routes but reprieving the line to Middlesbrough via the Esk Valley.

It was certainly an unusual choice. While the wonderfully scenic Esk Valley route serves several isolated villages, it was far from being the most direct link between Whitby and the main population of Yorkshire. Marples made his decision based on the importance of Whitby itself of retaining a rail service to connect it with the nearest large centre of population, the importance of the tourist trade to the port and the surrounding area and the extreme difficulty of operating buses over the Esk Valley roads, especially in winter.

As part of his campaign, the Labour candidate for Scarborough and Whitby produced a pledge signed by Harold Wilson himself that the remaining closures would not go ahead if his party won the election.

Within a month, Wilson was in Downing Street, ending more than 13 years of Conservative control, but had only a majority of four seats, and it was clear that Wilson would need to go to the polls again sooner rather than later to obtain a comfortable working majority.

How much the Beeching closures played in the downfall of the Conservative Government as opposed to, say, the Profumo scandal and the general mood of modernisation and a desire for change, drawing a line under the 'old order' once and for all, could not be calculated. Yet it was by no means a landslide in favour of those who pledged to stop the Beeching cuts; indeed, apart from the pledge, the closures barely featured in the election campaign.

Looked upon to redeem Labour's pre-election pledge with regard to Whitby, new Transport Minister Tom Fraser claimed that due to a technicality in the 1962 Transport Act, he was powerless to reverse his predecessor Marples' decisions, despite the fact that they had not yet been implemented. Neither did Wilson appear inclined to intervene with a state-controlled industry. The words 'cop-out' come quickly to mind, and instinctively begs the question – why does the electorate still heed election promises?

Yet there was no widespread uproar over the apparent U-turn. Maybe it was an indication that the new car-owning classes no longer had a reason to care about railways when they had discovered the new liberty that the open road gave them.

Also, many sections of the press were in support of Beeching's attempts to reduce the burden on the taxpayer by ridding the country of sizeable parts of a transport system which was by natural forces of supply and demand becoming obsolete. Indeed, *The Railway Magazine* had carried an editorial in its May 1963 issue which began: "Whether one agrees with all of 'the plan' or not, it has to be admitted that Dr Beeching's Report is basically correct and backed by such a weight of carefully prepared evidence as to be almost unassailable. It has been described as brutal, brilliant and right."

After turning his back on the promises to Whitby, Fraser authorised 39 out of 40 outstanding closures across the country. It appeared to be nothing less than a case of a seamless join with the Marples administration.

To many, this 'carry on as before' approach underlined the fact that some form of large-scale closure policy was viewed as inescapable on both sides of the political fence in a rapidly changing and modernising world. Therefore from this point of view at least, it is surely unfair or wrong to blame one or two individuals, Marples and Beeching, who found themselves in the time and place where circumstances dictated that they had to grasp the nettle in the first place.

The question is – could the problems of declining demand for rail services and the soaring deficit combined with streamlining the network to ensure its survival have been approached in a different way than that outlined in the Beeching report, and if so, would more or less closures have taken place? Could overall losses have been stemmed or reduced to an acceptable level, maybe by pruning operating costs to bare bones and running lines on a skeletal basis, or would it have been a case of sticking a finger in the dyke and putting off the evil day when far more drastic cutting back would have been inescapable?

The fact that sentimentality for railways did not even come bottom of the list of priorities, but did not feature at all in the Beeching report of 1963 is highlighted by the fact that the famous station at Llanfairpwllgwyngyllgogerychwyrndrobwllllantysiliogogogoch on the Bangor-Holyhead line was axed in 1966 along with most other stopping stations on the route in a bid to speed up journey times between primary destinations. ROBIN JONES

The name Llanfairpwllgwyngyllgogerychwyrndrobwllllantysiliogogogoch was created in the 1860s by a cobbler from Menai Bridge who dreamed it up so the station would have the honour of having the longest name of any in Britain, and encourage tourism. After the Britannia Bridge was destroyed by fire in 1970 severing the rail link, the station was reopened temporarily to allow local services to Holyhead. Then known simply as Llanfair PG, it opened in 1970, closed again in 1972 then reopened, firstly as Llanfairpwll, in 1973. In 1995, the station house was renovated and the main building rebuilt in 1993. ROBIN JONES

78 Beeching: 55 years of the Axe Man

A thermometer in the west

One stretch of British road became immortalised by traffic jams in the mid-20th century, firstly as car ownership and leisure time boomed, and secondly, as more car journeys were needed to replace closed railway branch lines to holiday resorts. The Exeter bypass.

The West Country has always been a choice destination for summer holidays, and Exeter was a hub both for journey by rail, with the Great Western and Southern rail lines from London meeting there, along with several of the main roads to both Devon and Cornwall.

By the 1920s, with the new car-owning middle class taking motoring holidays in the west, as opposed to travelling there by train, the city's streets were becoming overburdened, and several buildings had to be demolished for road widening and traffic lights first appeared in 1929. It was suggested that a new road should be built to take passing traffic around the town rather than through it.

Work began on an eastern bypass in the early 1930s, and the first section, from Bath Road west of Pinhoe to the Countess Wear roundabout, was completed by 1935. The section included the building of Gallows Bridge at Gallows Cross across the A30 London Road, with a slip road to allow traffic from London to join the bypass, and a roundabout where it crossed the road to Sidmouth at Middlemoor. Gallows Bridge was built from local red sandstone, and to the untrained eye, ironically looks every bit like a railway overbridge. Incidentally, the 'Gallows' recalled the place of execution at Heavitree where three Bideford women were hanged in 1682, when they became the last people in Britain to be documented as being executed for witchcraft.

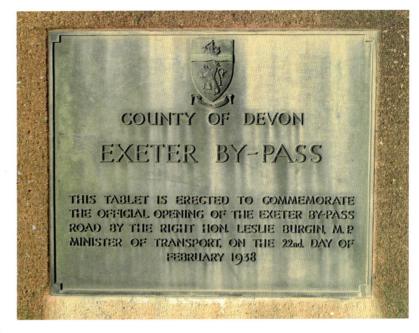

In August 1935, the building of the final section of the bypass between Countess Wear, running across the River Exe and Exeter Ship Canal to join the roads to Dawlish Road, Torquay and Plymouth began. It included a new swing bridge over the canal specially to accommodate the huge volumes of holiday traffic. This final section was opened by Transport Minister Leslie Burgin on February 22, 1938. The minister said: "The people of Exeter need have no fear of the bypass for it is better to have willing customers who can reach the city than disgruntled tourists who are delayed on their journeys through being unable to pass through it."

The plaque marking the opening of the Exeter bypass. ROBIN JONES

Gallows Bridge: you could be forgiven for thinking that it carries a railway rather than the Exeter bypass. ROBIN JONES

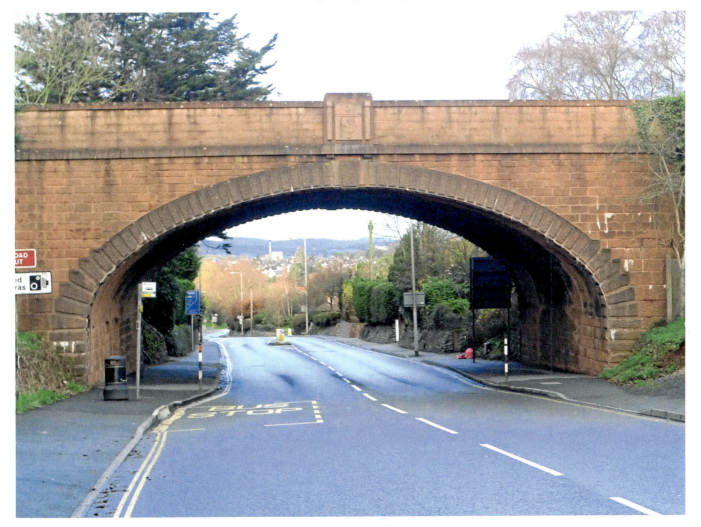

Beeching: 55 Years of the Axe Man **79**

The approach to the swing bridge taking the Exeter bypass over the Exeter Ship Canal. Deserted at breakfast time on a February morning, it was notoriously gridlocked during summer Saturdays in the 1950s and 60s.
ROBIN JONES

However, the bypass generated more disgruntled tourists than ever before by the mid-1950s, well before the great swathe of branch line closures began. Holiday specials still ran to the West Country resorts behind Great Western King 4-6-0s, but the motor car was rapidly seizing their crown, and queues on the bypass tailed back for hours at peak periods because it was not big enough to cope with the volume. Queues returned to Exeter city centre, as frustrated motorists tried to avoid the bypass. In a bid to address the problems in the summer of 1959, a raised platform was built in the centre of the Countess Wear roundabout, from which a policeman could manually control four sets of temporary traffic lights.

By the mid-1960s, rising car ownership combined with more resorts disenfranchised from the rail network saw 12-mile tailbacks on the Exeter bypass. By the summer of 1966 they were regularly making national news, as nearby the last rites were being read over branch line services. This situation, while individually notorious in terms of traffic congestion, may be viewed as a microcosm of the changing traffic patterns brought about by the great shift from rail to road, promoted by public demand and perpetuated by government transport policy.

The solution? Build more roads. In 1968, plans to extend the M5 south from Bristol to Exeter, bypassing the bypass, were announced. It was completed in October 1975, and included a new bridge built by British Rail for the surviving branch line to Exmouth.

The section of the bypass between the Countess Wear roundabout and Dawlish Road still generated traffic queues, at rush hour.

Slow Train

In 1963, the comic songwriting duo Michael Flanders and Donald Swann captured the mood of Britain with a song, Slow Train, about the Beeching cuts. Mentioning many stations including Trouble House Halt, later taken up by other artists including the King's Singers.
It ran as follows:

Miller's Dale for Tideswell ...
Kirby Muxloe ...
Mow Cop and Scholar Green ...

No more will I go to Blandford Forum and Mortehoe
On the slow train from Midsomer Norton and Mumby Road.
No churns, no porter, no cat on a seat
At Chorlton-cum-Hardy or Chester-le-Street.
We won't be meeting again
On the Slow Train.

I'll travel no more from Littleton Badsey to Openshaw.
At Long Stanton I'll stand well clear of the doors no more.
No whitewashed pebbles, no Up and no Down
From Formby Four Crosses to Dunstable Town.
I won't be going again
On the Slow Train.

On the Main Line and the Goods Siding
The grass grows high
At Dog Dyke, Tumby Woodside
And Trouble House Halt.

The Sleepers sleep at Audlem and Ambergate.
No passenger waits on Chittening platform or Cheslyn Hay.
No one departs, no one arrives
From Selby to Goole, from St Erth to St Ives.
They've all passed out of our lives
On the Slow Train, on the Slow Train.

Cockermouth for Buttermere ... on the Slow Train,
Armley Moor Arram ...
Pye Hill and Somercotes ... on the Slow Train,
Windmill End.

Several of these stations survived the Beeching Axe: Chester-le-Street, Formby, Ambergate and Arram, while Gorton & Openshaw is now just plain Gorton. The St Ives branch ended up being reprieved.

Lincolnshire's Tumby Woodside station, mentioned in the song Slow Train by Flanders and Swann, closed in 1970 and is pictured in 1981. Its canopy has since rotted away, but some of the crumbling brickwork is still apparent today.
DAVID BURROWS

GWR 4-6-0 No. 6003 *King George IV* stands at Wolverhampton Low Level, which closed to through trains in 1967 and completely in 1972.
BRIAN MORRISON

GWR 2-6-0 No. 7319 arrives at Ballingham with a Gloucester to Hereford via Ross-on-Wye train on May 20, 1964. Ballingham had a limited service and was never well used. It closed, along with the line, on November 2, 1964, under the Beeching Axe. The station building has been extended and is now a private house.
HUGH BALLANTYNE

The final Guildford-Horsham train, headed by 2-6-2 tank No. 41287, prepares to depart from Guildford on June 12, 1965. Three extra coaches were added to the journey, and chalked on the smokebox are 'The end-farewell' and on the side tank 'last day.'
P PAULTER/RM

Beeching: 55 Years of the Axe Man **81**

Chapter Eight

The whole world turns *blue*

Each of the 'Big Four' companies had its own corporate liveries for locomotives and rolling stock. British Railways tried to follow suit, but somehow struggled to get each of its regions to always agree.

The standard livery for most British Railway steam locomotives was black, while express passenger locomotives were painted in the Great Western colours of Brunswick green, with orange and black lining, irrespective of their 'Big Four' company of origin.

At one stage in the early Fifties, British Railways painted its express passenger locomotives in blue livery. Striking, yes, but practical, not at all: the livery was quick to show up dirt and grime at every available opportunity.

The livery met with a relatively early demise, but it was to remain, lurking around on a drawing board somewhere at British Railways HQ, ready for its moment again. That was to come with modernisation.

The first generation diesel multiple units and locomotives by and large appeared in green livery too, as if they were trying to be steam engines by the back door.

As part of a plan to find a suitable corporate livery for the then new diesel and electric fleet and coaching stock, several experiments were tried.

Class 31 diesel D5578 was painted in an unlined 'light electric blue' while sister D5579 took on a livery described as 'golden ochre'.

The first Class 52 Western class of diesel hydraulics, D1000 *Western Enterprise*, took on a pale brown livery known as 'desert sand' livery when first delivered in 1961. Sister D1015 *Western Champion* was delivered in a slightly different golden ochre to D5579,

Several Westerns and some of the Class 42 Warships were outshopped in maroon livery, to match the standard British Railways coaching livery. Meanwhile, the 25kv electric locomotives built for the East Coast Main Line were originally painted in a paler but brighter shade of blue known as 'electric blue.'

Meanwhile, shortly after nationalisation in 1948, it was decided that all coaches should be painted in a two-

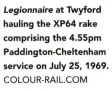

Class 52 D1029 *Western Legionnaire* at Twyford hauling the XP64 rake comprising the 4.55pm Paddington-Cheltenham service on July 25, 1969.
COLOUR-RAIL.COM

Preserved Class 52 diesel hydraulic D1062 *Western Courier,* seen on display on the West Somerset Railway's Minehead turntable in 2009, carries the British Railway maroon livery applied to some class members. ROBIN JONES

tone livery of carmine and cream for corridor coaches, with all-over crimson – very much as successor to the LMS livery – being used for local, non-corridor stock, to give a traditional 'feel' while differing from any of the 'Big Four' company liveries. In the Fifties came a relaxing on this 'one size fits all' rule, the regions were allowed to revert to liveries of their choice, with the most independent of them, the Western Region, readopting GWR chocolate and cream, while the Southern Region reverted to malachite green.

Carriages were repainted as and when they came in for overhaul, leaving trains running with an assortment of liveries – a situation worsened when vehicles from different regions became mixed together.

It would need a businessman to insist that a new national corporate livery was needed in order to dispense with the untidy and often tatty appearance of such 'mixed' trains, one in which locomotives would match passenger stock.

That man was Dr Beeching.

He saw that while passenger numbers of the railways were declining, rival forms of transport were upgrading their identities and services in an effort to stay ahead of the pack.

He decided that British Railways needed a major rebranding, from the locomotives and stock down to staff uniforms, station signs and even tableware, seat rest covers and official letterheads. It would highlight the improvements which had been made since the 1955 Modernisation Plan.

A new prototype train was to be produced, with improvements in internal equipment and décor, paving the way for future designs.

Spring collection: British Railways' new uniforms for its firemen, guards and drivers, introduced in early 1964. RM

The completion of the Western Region's switch from steam to diesel was heralded on 20 October 1965, when a new diesel serving and maintenances depot opened at the legendary steam shed of Old Oak Common. Pictured (from left) are Brush Co-Co D1719, north British diesel hydraulic D6353, a Western diesel hydraulic, Hymek diesel hydraulic D7065 and Brush Co-Co D1740. RM

Beeching: 55 Years of the Axe Man **83**

The unveiling of XP64

In May 1964, a train of eight new carriages, made up of three first class corridor coaches Nos M13407-9, two second class corridor coaches Nos M25508/9, and three open plan coaches No. M4727-9 rolled off the Derby production line.

Finished in a turquoise blue and pale grey livery with dark brown bogies and drawgear, the coaches were known as the Project XP64 stock.

The new coaches were designed to combine physical comfort and good appearance to a high degree, and give a smoother and quieter ride.

The improved smooth and silent running of the new trains was provided by the 'integral' method of building carriage frames, and a new carriage bogie, the B4 type, developed by the chief mechanical engineer's design staff. These developments aimed to save about five tons in the overall weight of each carriage.

The carriages were equipped with air heating and ventilation, improved sound proofing, 5ft-wide windows partially double-glazed, improved lighting, seats scientifically designed to be more restful, wider entrances with folding doors and wider steps – designed to improve access, especially for passengers carrying luggage or children. Compact, easy-to-clean toilet compartments featured two illuminated mirrors – one fitted above the wash basin with an electric razor point nearby, and the other giving full-length reflection– while the compartment also included a tip-up auxiliary seat.

Each of the three prototype first-class coaches had smoking and non-smoking compartments, and there were different decorations and colours for each one, making a total of six schemes.

At first, this new train was coupled behind a 'matching' Class 47diesel, D1733. Its colour scheme was matched to that of the coaches and revolutionised the appearance of the British Railways fleet.

The body was painted in the carriage's turquoise blue with the addition of a red square panel on the drivers' cabs to which was applied the 'new' network logo of two fused arrows – but more on that later.

The final layout of the logo was still being decided at this stage, and was shortly afterwards removed from the locomotive.

Small yellow warning panels were applied to the ends of the locomotives, and the numbers – two sets either side – placed directly behind the cabs, were in a new style font. The bogies and under frames again matched the coaching stock's brown.

Before widespread adoption, the shade of blue was slightly changed to a darker form, properly called 'monastral blue' and better known as 'rail blue'.

The XP64 coaches underwent demonstration runs between Marylebone and High Wycombe on May 28-29, 1964 and entered midweek service on the East Coast Main Line route between King's Cross and Edinburgh during the summer, made into a complete train by the addition of modern restaurant dining cars between the three first-class and one second-class coaches, with a standard second-class corridor brake at each end.

The year before, the prototype British Railways Mk2 coach, FK No 13252, was built. British Railways' second design of carriage, they had a semi-integral construction, giving it more strength than a Mk1 in the event of an accident, and the changed construction method overcame the serious corrosion problem point in the base of the Mk1s, where they were attached to the underframe. Other changes of design, such as the window units, were also made to reduce maintenance costs.

The Mk2s were introduced between 1964-66 and fitted with vacuum brakes, so they could run with Mk1 stock. A subsequent variation, the Mk2As, which appeared in 1967, was air braked only, and adopted many more features from the pioneer XP64 set.

Below: **Deltic No. 55015 *Tulyar*, an example of one of the finest classes of first-generation British diesels, departs from Lincoln with a King's Cross-Skegness railtour on Sunday, August 13, 1978.** BRIAN SHARPE

Class 47 diesel D1733 and the XP64 train, in experimental blue livery, without the red flash. COLOUR-RAIL.COM

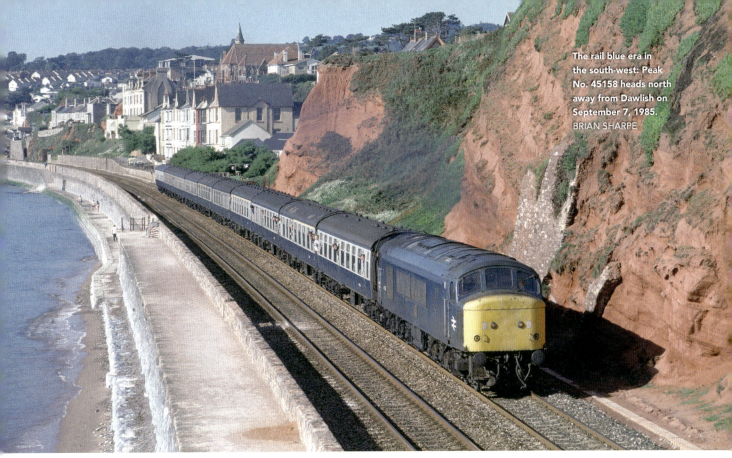

The rail blue era in the south-west: Peak No. 45158 heads north away from Dawlish on September 7, 1985. BRIAN SHARPE

From British Railways to British Rail

An exhibition 'The New Face of British Railways' was staged at the Design Centre in London from January 4-23, 1965, with the aim of launching British Railways 'corporate identity' programme.

Everything was to be painted in monastral blue and pearl grey, set off by flame red.

From the outset, locomotives kept the small yellow front warning panels from the green livery era, until the British Railways Board's accident prevention service ordered that the yellow was to cover the entire front of the cabs in order to make locomotives more visible to trackside staff for safety reasons.

Everything seen and used frequently by the public, every station, sign, and piece of printed matter, was to be given a recognisable family likeness.

One of the first applications of the new corporate livery was on British Railways ships: the hull was painted blue with a grey superstructure, while the black-topped funnel was red with the symbol in white.

The new corporate symbol, the finished double arrow, represented two-way rail service, and was simple enough to retain its impact when used in wide range of sizes and materials. Formed of two interlocked arrows, it was nicknamed 'the arrow of indecision'.

However, it would become one of the most successful corporate logos in history, long outliving British Railways and its rebranding as British Rail from January 1, 1965, and is still in use today on road signs indicating the way to stations, station signs themselves, and on printed rail tickets.

The new logotype was drawn to suit modern typography and used the abbreviation British Rail, the brand under which British Railways would henceforth operate.

Most freight rolling stock was not affected by the new colour scheme, with the yellow livery of the road freight transport, together with the recently-introduced freight symbol, retained.

The new, smart 'with it' (a classic mid Sixties phrase) modern uniforms were to be in general use through the network from spring 1966.

A rail freight employee pictured in April 1964. The photograph was taken during the making of the British Transport Films production A Corporate Identity. NRM

By 1966 blue and grey coaches were appearing on steam-hauled trains as well as behind diesel and electric locomotives. The colour was all but universally adopted by the 1970s, with some maroon coaches still awaiting their turn in the paint shops.

Three classes of diesels, the 20s, 25s and the 47s, were still in production when the livery change was decreed. D8178 became the first Class 20 to be outshopped from the start in rail blue as opposed to being repainted in it; D7660 was the first rail blue Class 25 and D1953 the first Class 47.

Incidentally one Class 20, D8048, appeared in rail blue livery with the double arrow symbols the wrong way round.

Deteriorating green liveries on many locomotives lasted into the mid-1970s. In November 1978, No. 47256 became the last Class 47 to be repainted into rail blue. Green Class 20s No. 20141 and 20147 were not repainted until July 1980 and may have been the last two locomotives to be reliveried.

Another aspect of the strict corporate image policy that marked a major break with that of the past was a ban on naming locomotives.

While the diesels that had been named in the early Sixties were left alone, everything had to have only a number.

In 1968, the numbering system was streamlined by the introduction of Total Operations Processing System, or TOPS, a US-developed computer system for managing the locomotives and rolling stock owned by a railway.

Up to the introduction of TOPS, steam locomotives carried numbers up to five digits long, diesels had carried three or four-digit numbers prefixed with the letter D, and electric locomotives with the letter E, meaning that in theory, three locomotives could carry the same number.

TOPS needed similar locomotives to be numbered in a consecutive series so they could be treated together as a group. Under the system the first two or three digits were used to denote the class of locomotive or multiple unit. Locomotives were designated classes 01–98: diesel locomotives 01–70, DC electric locomotives 71–79, AC electric locomotives 80–96, departmental locomotives 97, and steam locomotives 98… and British Rail's shipping fleet as Class 99. Around 500 diesel locomotives received TOPS numbers while still wearing green livery.

Was rail blue a success?

In time, everything was painted blue and grey. That may have been a great success in terms of corporate branding, but how did the general public view the new livery?

It was certainly a livery for the modern age, but was it the best choice of colour? While many were obviously impressed, there were those who felt it

The mid 1960s saw steam locomotives hauling rakes of blue and grey coaches intended for the diesel and electric era. In March 1968, Britannia Pacific No. 70013 *Oliver Cromwell* **heads a rake of blue and grey coaches out of Carnforth.**
DAVE RODGERS

lacked warmth and the character of the old 'Big Four' and regional liveries.

For them, rail blue was, and still is, symbolic of an age of mass pruning and rationalisation: the ripping out of the steam era infrastructure and the paring of everything that could be down to the bare bone. Setting aside the many route and station closures under Beeching, what survived was visibly rationalised. The use of diesel multiple units eliminated the need for run-round loops at termini, and many surviving branch lines, which had already lost their goods yards, became little more than long sidings.

One big effect of the Beeching report was the reduction of several double track sections of railway to single tracks, such as the route from Bicester to Princes Risborough, the Kyle of Lochalsh Line from Inverness to Dingwall, and the LSWR's West of England Main Line west of Salisbury.

There were cases where road building schemes were given priority over railways to the point where routes were singled; a classic example is the Chester to Wrexham General line which has a dual carriageway bridge on the A483 over the railway where space was left for only one track. Such singling led to bottlenecks during the rail traffic resurgence experienced in Britain from the 1980s onwards.

Weeds grew amid the flagstones of platforms left devoid of passengers and track, and where many stations and halts remained in use, their Victorian buildings and expensive-to-maintain wooden canopies were pulled down and replaced with bus shelters, or in several instances no shelters at all. That begged the question – had modern man evolved to the point where, unlike his Victorian forebears, he was prepared to stand outside in all weathers waiting for trains?

British Rail adhered rigidly to the all-in-blue policy until 1976, when a few chinks of light in the wall appeared, with the introduction of the first InterCity 125 High Speed Train and its modified form of the livery, with yellow from the front extended along the side of each power car, although the coaches retained the usual rail blue coaching stock colours.

Further variants followed, and with the sectorisation of the eighties, different liveries altogether appeared, such as the Railfreight grey with yellow ends.

Privatisation wiped away rail blue, which is now confined to the heritage sector. Many modern traction enthusiasts who grew up with it adore it: for those who remember what went before, many see the all-pervading blue as a kind of anaesthetic and representative of a regime that purged the railways of everything that went before, regardless of any ill side effects.

Below: **The Portsmouth-Cardiff services were among BR's last regular locomotive-hauled cross-country services, such as No. 33015 seen at Claverton on April 24, 1988.** BRIAN SHARPE

Left: **Another locomotive-hauled cross country service was from Norwich to Birmingham. No 31455 passes Manton Junction, where the line joins the one-time St Pancras-Nottingham main line, on 2 May 1988.** BRIAN SHARPE

Left: **Towards the end of the last year of locomotive-hauled services on the West Highland extension to Mallaig, No 37408 drops downhill from Arisaig past Kinloid on 28 October 1987.** BRIAN SHARPE

Chapter Nine

Beeching Mark 2!

In terms of eradicating the British Railways deficit, Beeching's plan of 1963 failed.

By axing nearly a third of the rail network, he achieved savings of just £30 million, yet overall losses were still running in excess of £100 million.

Despite the figures for savings he had promised in his report, as far as the given examples were concerned, the contrary was happening, the fact that loss-making branch lines acted as feeders to the main lines could not be escaped. Indeed, closing branch lines meant less traffic on loss-making main lines which then became themselves at risk.

Also, while many of the closed lines recorded only a small operating deficit, they were still recommended for the axe. When it fell, the savings their closures contributed were a drop in the ocean to the overall scheme of things.

While the motorway network was expanding, the railway freight network was rapidly receding, with the closure of branch lines and the elimination of the pick-up goods. Rather than lorries taking goods to the nearest railhead for onward transhipment to another freight yard, where they would be collected again by lorry, it was easier, cheaper and far more convenient for a road haulier to do the job from start to finish. With the introduction of containerisation, this job was made easier for lorries. It is highly debatable as to whether Beeching placed sufficient emphasis on this aspect back in 1963.

The problem with sending freight by rail is that the end user ideally should also be rail connected. For instance, one of the biggest volumes of freight on the network comprised

coal, taken straight from the mines to stations on every main and branch line, many of which would have a coal merchant based next door. Householders would be able to buy supplies of coal for heating straight from the rail yard.

However, this ceased to be the case when branch lines closed, and the supplier was cut off from rail access to markets. At the same time, coal was increasingly being replaced as a primary source of domestic heating by gas, electricity and oil, and more homes were being built or modernised with central heating. The emergence of natural gas by the Seventies as a mainstream form of domestic heating dealt a crushing blow for coal traffic.

As the railways expanded in the 19th century, heavy industry sprang up alongside rail lines, with goods being shipped in and out of private sidings. However, if the end user was not connected, road would be the only viable alternative.

It is easy to ask today why this quarry or that foundry does not use rail, and increase environmental benefits, but it does not automatically make economic sense when the freight has to be offloaded from rail and on to road somewhere down the line.

Similarly, as stated earlier Beeching appeared to assume that if a branch line was closed, passenger would simply drive to the nearest main line station. Most of them, it seemed, decided not to bother, and make the whole journey in their car.

Replacing branch line trains with theoretically more versatile bus services was far from overwhelming success. Many bus routes were slower and less convenient than the trains they had replaced, while others simply ran between the closed railway stations, offering no advantage over the train.

Many replacement bus services only lasted a few years before they too were withdrawn due to lack of use, leaving large tracts of the countryside without public transport, and forcing people who had previously relied on it to buy cars.

Beeching's 1965 report did not name the East Coast Main Line between Newcastle-upon-Tyne to Edinburgh, seen here at Burnmouth, as a preferred trunk route – leading to grave concerns that it could have been closed.
BRIAN SHARPE

Manchester Piccadilly in the final stages of rebuilding in 1964. Beeching's 1965 report would have concentrated resources on trunk routes, leaving critics to fear the rest would be closed. RM

A second bite at the cherry

In February 1965, British Railways published a second Beeching report, titled *The Development of the Major Railway Trunk Routes*.

Dubbed 'Beeching II', the report picked out routes which would justify large-scale investment to handle projected increases in both passenger and freight traffic over the next two decades.

At first glance, it appeared highly positive, with major investment in a series of identified key routes.

However, many critics immediately saw this as 'spin', masking the fact that the routes that were not to be chosen for upgrading would sooner or later end up being closed, and sounded their fears for the worst.

Beeching denied that drastic closures were top of his new agenda in the closing paragraphs of the conclusion to the 1965 report.

He stated: "For the sake of clarity, it is emphasised that non-selection of lines for intensive development does not necessarily mean that they will be abandoned in the foreseeable future, nor even that money will not be spent upon some of them to improve their suitability for their continuing purpose.

"It is emphasised that the developed trunk lines will be supported by several thousand miles of freight feeder lines, and that clarification of the position with regard to trunk route development will facilitate decisions about the feeder network. It is also emphasised that the provision of capacity for commuter traffics into the main urban areas is the subject of separate consideration."

Many still remained unconvinced by Beeching's assurances. If their fears had been realised, little more than 3000 miles of 'primary route' would have been left after the others were closed.

Wales would have been left without any British Railways service apart from the Great Western Main Line as far as Swansea, and nothing would have run in Scotland apart from the central belt services and the lines to Fife and Aberdeen.

The East Coast Main Line could have been truncated at Newcastle-upon-Tyne and Scotland-bound trains rerouted to Carlisle, from which only one route would have headed over the border.

There would have been no services west of Plymouth, while much of Yorkshire and East Anglia would have lost their services too. Norwich would still be linked to London, but Cambridge would be without any railway. Lines in Kent and Sussex may also have gone leaving only Brighton, Dover and Folkestone connected to the capital.

The report foresaw a reduction of more than 50% in the existing network of 7500 route miles between the main centres of population and industry, cutting them to around 3000 miles, by addressing and rationalising 3700 miles of duplicated' routes, 700 miles of triplicated and 700 miles of quadruplicated lines, a legacy from the days of the Railway Mania.

This pruning would save approximately £85 million on annual system maintenance and another £100 million on new locomotives, rolling stock, signalling and other infrastructure.

The British Railways Board also denied that the 1965 report was "a prelude to closures on a grand scale", but the fact that its implementation would lead reduced maintenance based on a systematic, if gradual, reduction of much of the main line network again provided much ammunition to those who claimed it was another swathe of closures by the back door.

While basing Beeching II on an assessment of the likely volume and traffic patterns between then and 1984, the doctor also accepted that periodic reappraisals would be both necessary and desirable.

The report claimed that the ultimate choice lies between "an excessive and increasingly uneconomic system, with a corresponding tendency for the railways as a whole to fall into disrepute and decay, or the selective development and intensive utilisation of a more limited trunk route system".

The cost of providing the railway track and signalling per unit of traffic passing over it must be reduced to a level which enables services to be provided on a competitive basis, the report argued.

It was proposed that trains should be grouped according to speed. Coal and minerals would move at an average of 35mph, oil and general merchandise at 50mph and passengers at either 50 or 70mph. 70% of all trains would travel at 50mph, although alternative routes would be used for faster and slower trains.

The routes chosen for upgrading were:

For traffic between London and Birmingham, London and Manchester/Liverpool, London and Scotland: Selected route – the West Coast Main Line from Euston via Rugby, Crewe, Preston and Carlisle; Rejected routes – the Great Central line from Marylebone through Leicester, Nottingham and Sheffield and the former Great Western line from Paddington through High Wycombe and Banbury.

For traffic between London and the East Midlands, South Yorkshire and the Tyne-Tees area: Selected route – the East Coast Main from King's Cross via Peterborough, York, Newcastle-upon-Tyne; Rejected routes – the Great Central line and the line through Cambridge, March, Spalding and Lincoln, joining the East Coast Main Line at Doncaster.

For traffic between London and Leeds, Sheffield, Nottingham and Leicester: Selected route – the Midland Main Line, from St Pancras through Leicester, Nottingham and Sheffield; Rejected route – the Great Central line.

For traffic between London, South Wales and the South-west: Selected route – the Great Western line from Paddington through Reading and Swindon, dividing at Wootton Bassett for South Wales via the Severn Tunnel and Bristol via Bath; Rejected routes – the line from Paddington through Newbury and Taunton and the line from Waterloo through Basingstoke, Salisbury and Yeovil.

For traffic between the north east and south west: Selected route – the line through Leeds, Sheffield, Derby, Burton, Birmingham and Gloucester; Rejected routes – the line from Leeds through Manchester, Crewe, Shrewsbury and Hereford and the line between Birmingham, Stratford-upon-Avon, Honeybourne and Gloucester.

For traffic across the Pennines: Selected routes – the line from Leeds to Manchester via Hebden Bridge and the electrified line from Sheffield to Manchester via Woodhead.

Rejected routes – the lines from Leeds to Manchester via Diggle, from Sheffield to Manchester via the Hope Valley and from Derby to Manchester via the Peak.

For traffic between Southampton and the Hampshire area and the Midlands: Selected route – the line from Southampton through Reading, Didcot and Banbury to Birmingham.

For traffic between Glasgow and Edinburgh: Selected route – the line via Falkirk and Polmont.

The report predicted a four per cent annual increase in the level of trunk route traffic over the coming 20 years. The general spread of industrial activity was also taken as remaining the same as at present – not foreseeing the mass closures of heavy industry such as coal mines and steelworks in the Eighties.

The total volume of trunk freight movement was expected to double by 1984, but a decline in rail passenger travel is anticipated, particularly on stopping services on main lines. "Most of them are grossly under-used and hopelessly uneconomic now and are likely to become more so in future because of road improvement and further growth in car ownership," the report said, adding that the railways did not expect to compete with the private car over distances of less than 100 miles where "the railways could not expect to retain a great part of this traffic by fare reductions". Air travel was also seen as a major competitor to long-distance passenger services having the advantage of speed.

A refocus on providing bulk transport over routes of heavy demand and over medium to long distances with frequent services at high speeds and offering a high standard of comfort was seen as the answer to keeping fares at a competitive level.

"There is no doubt that, on the assumptions outlined in the report, an expanding market exists for both freight and passenger transport," the report said. "Nevertheless, the volume of railway traffic has been declining, and it follows that the railway share of the total traffic has been falling even faster.

"The railways must reshape, and redeploy their assets and service, so as to concentrate on cheap bulk movement, if the decline is to be arrested and reversed. The railways will then play their full part in helping forward the pace of industrial growth itself.

"If the railways concentrate on cheap bulk movement, their prospects as trunk carriers can be revived. The danger is that failure to change, to modernise and to concentrate, will cause the present decline to continue.

"This study provides a basis for positive planning. Once the lines most likely to form the trunk rail network during the next 20 years have been determined, the railways will be better able to develop routes, operating methods, and services, to cater for the main traffic flows of the country at economic prices. It will also be possible to concentrate railway investment upon the selected trunk routes in the confidence that, on this railway of the future, the essential dense flows of traffic will be maintained."

Many of the critics who had read between the lines of the 1965 Report remained unmoved.

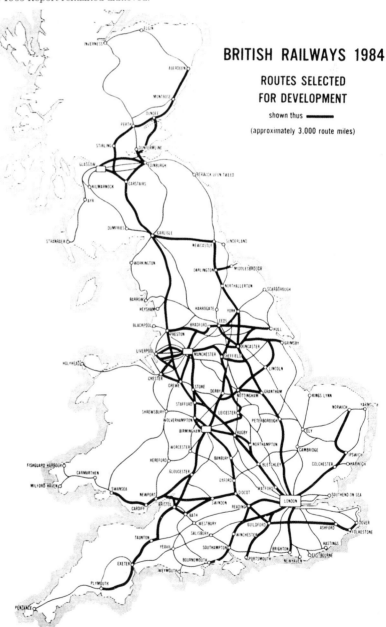

The trunk routes earmarked for investment in Beeching's 1965 report. Critics swiftly rounded on it and said that the remaining lines would end up being closed.

Beeching: 55 Years of the Axe Man **91**

Was the doctor 'struck off' the railways?

During 1964, Beeching has raised the issue of the comparative costs of transport freight by rail and road on several occasions and said that it needed to be determined as soon as possible. It was being said at the time that road haulage was not paying its full share of the costs of the trunk roads that had driven many railways to close.

Figures, Beeching argued, were needed so that the best combination of methods to provide the best service at the lowest costs could accurately be determined.

By then, he had made many enemies and few admirers, especially among the trade unions. His latest angered the road lobby, but Beeching was not taking sides here: he merely wanted a decision based on facts, whether road or rail would be the winner

Beeching had been asked by the Government to take on a new role, one in which he would carry out such a study to integrate Britain's entire transport system.

Beeching said he was willing to carry out the task but could devote no more than six months to it, as he intended to return to ICI as agreed.

The Government wanted him to carry out his study in conjunction with both the management and unions, but Beeching insisted that he preferred to work on his own. After several meetings with Harold Wilson, the Prime Minister decided that Beeching would have to accept assessors representing the road lobby… as – what may come as a surprise to many – he was considered to be too pro rail!

Beeching and the Government could not agree terms despite much discussion, and the job offer was withdrawn.

So did he decide to leave British Railways of his own accord, on May 31, 1965, or was he pushed out of his £24,000-a-year job, a year before his five-year leave period from ICI was due to expire? The question has never been satisfactorily resolved.

In a statement to the House of Commons, Transport Minister Tom Fraser said: "Since it is Dr Beeching's desire to return to ICI by the middle of next year, I have come to the conclusion that it would not be practicable for him to carry out the sort of study the government want, in the way in which we think it should be done, during the time which he could devote to it."

He added that he would welcome Dr Beeching's advice during his remaining time at British Railways.

However, Frank Cousins, the Labour minister of technology, told the Commons in November 1965 that Beeching had been sacked by Fraser, the man who the following month introduced the 70mph speed limit on motorways as an emergency measure following a series of multiple crashes in fog.

Beeching denied both at the time and until his death that he had been dismissed, highlighting the fact that he had returned early to ICI as he would not have had enough time to undertake an in-depth transport study before the formal end of his secondment.

So he was not openly sacked, but neither was he openly backed, even though senior government figures including Barbara Castle and even Prime Minister, Harold Wilson, privately agreed with his prognosis for Britain's transport network.

In 1965, Beeching was rewarded for his years of public service by being made a life peer as Baron Beeching of East Grinstead in the Queen's Birthday Honours List.

A sight which would have delighted Beeching who wanted rid of steam as soon as possible: Stanier 8F 2-8-0 No. 48278 is turned on the Rose Grove turntable after performing the final steam banking duty at Copy Pit on August 3, 1968. TERRY FLINDERS

Crowds surround Britannia Pacific No. 70013 *Oliver Cromwell* as it took over the '15 Guinea Special' At Manchester Victoria for the next leg to Carlisle on August 11, 1968. This tour marked the end of British Rail steam haulage on the national network.
PETER FITTON

Beeching successor: a backer or backtracker?

Beeching was replaced as chairman of British Railways by a figure from within the rail industry. Stanley Raymond had joined the Western Region as divisional manager in 1962 and had impressed with his hard work to reduce soaring losses.

In a paper read to the Institute of Transport in spring 1966, Raymond said: "The problem is to decide how essential and how convenient, and what are the rules under which the railway services are to be provided."

With regard to Beeching's 1965 report, he said that since its publication, a detailed examination had been made of the feeder services that would be required to sustain the proposed 3000-trunk route system and this, together with a reconsideration of some of the original proposals in the 1963 report, would add up to 9000 route miles which, along the commuter services which needed separate consideration, form the framework of the modern railway which the British Railways Board "now believes should be developed in the national interest".

While he far from condemned the Beeching closures, it became apparent that it was now seen that the steamroller set in motion by the doctor should stop.

Stanley said: "It seems clear that substantial sections of the nation are not ready to face up to the consequences of the streamlining of the railways to the full extent required by present legislation – to enable the railways to eliminate their deficit. While the stage of saying 'this is the end of closures; can never be reached, because of the rapidly changing industrial scene and technological advance, it is feasible to establish a watershed and show a network of routes, services and facilities that substantially should remain for the foreseeable future.

"Such a network might involve closing 2000 or so route miles over which passenger services now operate, most of which has already been announced, and a further 1500 or so miles which carry freight traffic only. This would leave the 11,000/12,000 route miles of trunk and feeder lines already referred to.

"This network would be much greater than the 8000 route miles which, at one time, were in mind."

He echoed Beeching when he said that to the maximum extent possible, stopping passenger services would be removed from the main lines enabling the railways to concentrate on the operation of through and limited-stop fast passenger services between main centres of industry and population. "Fast and reliable freight services would be operated over this new streamlined network to link all main industrial areas and ports and give proper road/rail interchange facilities," he said.

Talking about urban commuter lines, he said that passenger services within the principal conurbation areas of London and the South East, Manchester, Liverpool, Glasgow, Birmingham, Tyneside and Teesside, West Yorkshire and Cardiff performed a unique function for the community. "It is now generally accepted throughout the world that suburban operations of this kind cannot be performed profitably on a commercial basis," he said. "Nor is there any form of transport yet devised to replace the function of the suburban railway services.

"The great transport issue today is not the old one of road v rail, but the new one of public transport v private transport, and what is the level of public transport which the nation requires and is prepared to pay for? But a balance must soon be struck and decisions made as to the future size and shape of the railway system so as to give a degree of stability to the industry and allow railway management to concentrate more on their prime task of running trains and providing a service."

He said that the changes and service cuts made under Beeching "were essential to sweep away the clutter of the past so that clear decisions can be made for the future". But again, he reiterated that it was now time to bring the rail closures to an end and determine what railway network should be set in stone, even if it meant subsidising lines for social reasons.

"We are now rapidly approaching a watershed and it will be in the best interests of the nation and of the industry if that watershed is determined, the remaining doubtful services eliminated, and energies devoted to making the substantial system that remains efficient and a national asset.

"But it must be emphasised that the system outlined will still have the capacity to provide a large element of standby transport for the users of private transport when it suits their convenience. This standby transport capacity will have to be paid for. It is essential that the preoccupation with the deficit and the administrative and planning work connected with the reshaping and streamlining should not monopolise the efforts of management."

Beeching: 55 Years of the Axe Man **93**

Chapter Ten

More closures,
followed by compassion

On December 23, 1965, Barbara Castle was appointed as transport minister. She became famous as the person who introduced the breathalyser to tackle the rising problem of drink-driving, and also made the 70mph motorway speed limit permanent.

She was behind legislation that ruled that all cars had to be fitted with seat-belts.

Furthermore, she oversaw the closure of around 2050 miles of railway lines both under the Beeching plan along with routes that the doctor had not prescribed, such as Buxton to Matlock, and so her appointment was in that respect far from a U-turn.

However, under her 1968 Transport Act, she importantly introduced a new social factor into legislation regarding such closures, and a further 3500 miles were given the possibility of a reprieve.

While, as we have already seen, the Labour government under Wilson had reneged big time on its 1964 pre-election pledge to halt the Beeching cuts, it had become increasingly apparent that not only had the rail closures not produced anything like the promised savings or ended the British Railways deficit but were unlikely ever to do so.

Castle recognised that while many services earmarked for closure were unremunerative, they nonetheless played a vital social role, and if they closed, the communities they served would suffer hardship.

Her first role in the government had been as the first minister for overseas development, and she was only the fourth woman in history ever to hold position in a British cabinet.

She had hoped to win a bigger seat in the cabinet, and at first did not want the transport portfolio (she could not even drive) but Wilson told her that he needed a 'tiger in the tank' in that department, quoting the Esso petrol advertising slogan of the day.

However, once appointed, she quickly warmed to the challenge.

By 1966, the year when the Exeter bypass was making even bigger summer headlines than ever before, roads were carrying 90% of passenger mileage and 60% of freight ton mileage. However, the laws regarding road safety had not caught up with the great switch from rail, while urban areas were creaking under the weight of the upsurge in traffic.

That year, 8000 people died on the roads. 'One for the road' drivers could drink as much as they liked and drive as fast as they liked.

Castle's subsequent 1967 Road Safety Act saved lives. It brought in not only the breathalyser but a year's ban for those who failed it. At the end of the first five months of its use, it was estimated that 800 lives had been saved by it.

Not everyone liked the idea: she was even sent a death threat by an angry motorist.

However, while realising that the car was now king and would stay so, she wanted to see a new integrated transport policy that not only accepted that fact but would breathe new life into public transport, particularly in urban areas where congestion was making its mark. That would have to include, as Stanley Raymond had stated following the departure of Beeching, subsidies to commuter lines.

She said: "I refused to be a King Canute trying to force people onto railways which could not take them where they wanted to go.

"If the private car had brought the boon of mobility to millions of people, which it clearly had, then that boon should be available to everyone. We must collectively face the consequences and deal with them through new arrangements which reflected the new facts."

Despite some successes of modernisation such as the Freightliner container trains, British Rail could not make its still-enormous freight system pay its way, when faced with stiffening competition from lorry transport.

Castle tried to introduce balance by having road hauliers soak up more of the expense they imposed on the roads. She also improved road haulage safety standards, by introducing the tachograph which limited drivers' daily hours – a move by which the left-winger aroused deep anger from the trade unions.

94 *Beeching: 55 Years of the Axe Man*

A new National Freight Corporation would encompass Freightliner and British Rail's remaining road freight services to create a streamlined competitive single unit, again provoking the fury of the Transport & General Workers Union.

While railway closures rolled on at a very high rate, she saved several individual routes including branch lines; York to Harrogate, Manchester to Buxton, Oxenholme to Windermere, Exeter to Exmouth and in Cornwall, the Looe branch and the St Ives line.

With regard to the latter two, Barbara Castle called Beeching's plans "slaughter of the innocents" and described the St Erth to St Ives as the most beautiful coastal journey in the country.

The Looe branch was saved because of the difficult winding roads serving the resort. Mrs Castle said: "In spite of the financial savings to the railways, it just wouldn't have made sense in the wider context to have transferred heavy holiday traffic on to the roads which couldn't cope with it.

"Nor would extensive and expensive road improvements have been the answer. At St Ives, these would have involved destroying the whole character of the town. At Looe, they could not have avoided long delays in the holiday season.

"It would have been the economics of Bedlam to spend vast sums only to create greater inconvenience."

In a similar vein, part of the Bere-Alston to Callington branch was saved, because of the hilly terrain at the point where the rivers Tamar and Tavy meet and the circuitous road routes. The branch was truncated at Gunnislake, and the Section of the Southern railway's Plymouth-Exeter main line which was lifted in 1968 was retained as far north as Bere Alston. A new station was built at Gunnislake in 1994.

She also spared Hope and Edale stations on the Manchester-Chinley-Sheffield line, which served in the Peak District National Park. However, at the same time, she allowed the closure of the Buxton-Matlock route to passengers: since the early Seventies, revivalists under the banner of Peak Rail have been trying to rebuild it.

As minister, Barbara Castle tackled the problem of financing the railways, and wrote off more than a billion pounds of British Rail's debt.

She introduced the means by which both national and regional government would be able to subsidise lossmaking parts of the network that nonetheless provided wider social and economic benefits.

Section 39 of the 1968 Act introduced the first Government subsidies for such lines. Grants could be paid where three conditions were met.

Firstly, the line had to be unremunerative. Secondly, it was desirable for social or economic reasons for the passenger services to continue, and thirdly, it was financially unreasonable to expect British Rail to provide those services without a grant.

Barbara Castle: introduced the breathalyser test while minister of transport.
PASSENGER TRANSPORT EXECUTIVE GROUP

A Royal Mail stamp issued in 2008 celebrating the life of Barbara Castle MP.

On September 21, 2008, Transport Secretary Ruth Kelly joined the family of Barbara Castle to help name a Northern Rail train after the late Labour MP and first woman transport minister, to mark the 40th anniversary of the 1968 Transport Act. Castle's niece Sonya Hinton (picture above) unveiled her name on the train at the ceremony, organised by the Passenger Transport Executive Group, at Manchester Oxford Road station. PET chairman Neil Scales said: "In many ways Barbara Castle was the most far-sighted transport minister that Britain has ever had. In the mid-Sixties she recognised that creating locally accountable strategic transport authorities for the conurbations would be essential if her wider aims for a planned and integrated national transport policy were to be achieved. In doing so she gave our cities a template which still guides us today." NORTHERN RAIL

The Act saved several branch lines from closure, but some, like the aforementioned Waverley Route and the Barnstaple-Ilfracombe line, still did not qualify under criteria and were axed as Beeching intended. Indeed, the Varsity Line that linked the university cities of Oxford and Cambridge saw services withdrawn from the Oxford-Bletchley section and the Bedford-Cambridge section at the end of 1967, even though the line had not been listed for closure in Beeching's 1963 report.

By the time the 1968 Transport Act had been passed, many lines and services and railway lines that would have qualified for subsidies had already been closed, making it a case of shutting the stable door after the horse had bolted.

While this approach was a marked change from the Beeching report of 1963, in fairness the doctor had never been given a social factor remit of this type, and had been told to make whatever moves he saw fit on a financial basis to eliminate the railways' rapidly-worsening deficit. From that view, it might be considered unfair to criticise Beeching's findings in themselves, as opposed to the implementation of them by Ernest Marples.

Castle's approach to subsiding railways has continued to this day.

Yet it was not only railways that were by now suffering financially. The remaining private bus companies, some of which had put the branch lines out of business, were also struggling against rising car ownership. The 1968 Act placed more of the national bus network under the National Bus Company, formed from January 1, 1969, by merging the bus operating companies of the Government-owned Transport Holding Company with those of the privately-owned British Electric Traction Company Limited, a large nationwide conglomerate, while fuel subsidies were increased and a fleet replacement grant introduced. Licensing for mini-buses was eased and a rural bus grant introduced.

For the cities, the Act legislated for integrated public transport networks to be set up: the Greater London Council would take over London Transport and elsewhere, new Passenger Transport Executives would be set up. These would have wide-ranging powers to integrate local road and rail services, running local buses and harmonising with British Rail on commuter fares and services.

Sixties icon the Midland Pullman waits at Platform 6 at Manchester Central station on October 6, 1965. This service was discontinued with the start of full electric services between Piccadilly and Euston on April 15, 1966. Rationalisation saw Manchester Central downgraded in favour of Manchester Piccadilly; Barbara Castle's closure of Matlock-Buxton meant that it saw even less use, and it finally closed to passengers on May 5, 1969. Its ruin used as a car park for a decade, in 1986 it reopened as G-MEX, the Greater Manchester Exhibition and Conference Centre, later renamed Manchester Central because of its railway history.
JOHN CLARKE/RM

Barbara Castle saved the St Ives branch from closure, and on May 27, 1978 Lelant Saltings station was opened to provide a park and ride facility for visitors to the often-congested resort arriving by car. First Great Western Class 150 diesel multiple unit No. 150221 leaving with 1.25pm to St Erth. FGW

Passenger services were withdrawn from the GWR Cinderford branch in November 1958, but the town station remained in use as a goods depot until August 1967. In July 1967, a pair of sheep wander on to little Cinderford Bridge Halt long deserted by passengers. GREAT WESTERN SOCIETY

Left: **During the electrification of the West Coast Main Line by British Railways, the GWR's Birmingham Snow Hill handled most of the rail traffic through the city, but overall, the Beeching closure programme took the view that Snow Hill station, seen here in the 1960s, was 'doubling up', and all services were switched to New Street and Moor Street. Long distance services through Snow Hill were cut in 1967 and the tunnel beneath the city centre from the south was closed to all traffic.** BEN BROOKSBANK/ CREATIVE COMMONS

The modern terminus at Gunnislake comprises a platform and bus shelter, a far cry from the days when Dr Beeching was presented with gross overstaffing at stations on many lossmaking rural branch lines. Incidentally, at Callington, the original terminus of the branch, there is now a Beeching Business Park named after the axe wielder. GEOFF SHEPPARD/CREATIVE COMMONS

The Marples-era weighting towards road building was eradicated with the capital grant regime adjusted so that public transport as well as roads projects, could benefit from 75% capital grants.

It was not just railways facing route closures in the Sixties. Their predecessors, the canals were also being prepared for mass pruning.

As a point of clarification, it is often assumed that railways killed off the canals. This was certainly true in some cases, but the inland waterway network lived on alongside the railways until well into the 20th century.

It was the big freeze of 1962/63 which by and large sounded the death knell for large-scale freight traffic on canals, when barges were left frozen into position for several weeks.

In 1967, the Government wanted to close canals to save money, but Barbara Castle managed to stave off the threat. She kept closures on the 1400 mile network to a minimum while reclassifying canals into commercial and leisure categories, recognising that pleasure boating was on the up. She said that her approach promised "new hope for those who love and use our canals, whether for cruising, angling or just walking on the towpath, or who want to see stretches of canal in some of our unlovely built-up areas, developed as centres of beauty or fun".

Both the Conservative opposition and trade unions fought hard against the Bill for the 1968 Act, with Enoch Powell even telling the House of Commons that it was 'evil'.

Despite around 2500 amendments and a record 45 committee sittings, Castle refused to water down her proposals, and her stance made her, according to opinion polls, the most popular minister in Wilson's Government, which for various reasons had by then lost much favour with the public.

Her success as transport minister led to her being moved to the role of minister for employment before the Bill was completed, but not before British Rail chairman Stanley Raymond was forced to resign in late 1967 following a disagreement with her, and received a settlement of £28,000 as he was contracted to serve until 1970.

Left: **Despite the fact it served a sizeable town, British Railways closed Alfreton station on Derbyshire's Erewash Valley line in 1967. However, it reopened in 1973, as Alfreton and Mansfield Parkway, as nearby Mansfield was by then, thanks to Beeching, the largest town in Britain without a station. It reverted to plain Alfreton in 1995.** MIDLAND RAILWAY TRUST

While the mid to late Sixties brought a reprieve for some of the GWR branch lines in the South West listed by Beeching, there was no let off for branches which formed part of the rival Southern Railway's sprawling and very winding 'Withered Arm' west of Exeter, leading to claims that old scores between rival companies were settled once they passed into Western Region hands.

Despite dieselisation, the last trains to Padstow, the westernmost extremity of the Southern Railway, ran on January 30, 1967. The station building and its platform survives as the town council offices, while a preserved milepost outside the Shipwrights Arms on North quay indicates the distance to Waterloo.

The line to Bude closed on October 3, 1966, also sounding the end for Halwill Junction, where the North Cornwall Railway route to Launceston and Padstow and the line to Torrington diverged. A housing estate stands near the site of the station, on a road named Beeching Close.

The twin East Devon branches to Sidmouth and Budleigh Salterton lost their passenger services on March 6, 1967.
ROBIN JONES/NRM

It's getting better

Raymond, later Sir Stanley Raymond, was replaced as British Rail chairman by Sir Henry (Bill) Johnson, who had joined the London & North Eastern Railway and rose through the ranks to become general manager of the London Midland Region in 1958 and its chairman in 1963-7. He took charge of the electrification of the Euston to Manchester and Liverpool line, and the development of new Euston station.

Railway finances improved under Johnson, largely as a result of the 1968 Transport Act, in which the government promised grants to prop up loss-making passenger services where they were providing a public service.

InterCity, started in 1966 as a branded operation of high-speed trains linking major cities, expanded, and in 1969 work began at the Derby Research Centre on the Advanced Passenger Train.

He took charge of the commercial development of surplus railway land, which realised £20-million a year for British Railways in the Seventies. He made progress towards improving industrial relations and despite the cutbacks which continued under Labour, he was popular with railway staff, many of who saw him as one of their own.

He was appointed CBE in 1962, knighted in 1968, and became KBE in 1972, the year after he stepped down from railways.

Chapter Eleven

The end of mass closures

By the early Seventies, the map of the British Rail network looked very much as it does today.

In 1970, 275 miles were closed, followed by 23 in 1971, 50 in 1972, 35 in 1973 and none in 1974.

By then, all the blatant lossmakers for which there were no social arguments to keep open had gone, and it was becoming increasingly clear that closures were having a negative impact.

The small amount of money saved by closing a line was outweighed by the increasing road congestion and pollution from motor vehicle exhausts.

One shock closure on January 5, 1970 which stood out from the rest was that of the 1500V DC electrified Woodhead Route between Sheffield and Manchester. The electrification had been completed in 1955 when the upgraded line was opened amid a blaze of publicity.

Its controversial closure just 15 years later, and for which Beeching was not responsible, came after it was decided that the alternative Hope Valley line through Edale would be to stay open instead, for social and network reasons, and would accommodate all Manchester-Sheffield passenger traffic. The Woodhead Route's Class 77 locomotives for passenger traffic were sold to the Netherlands Railways.

The line remained open for freight, mainly coal trains from Yorkshire to Fiddlers Ferry power station near Widnes which required a switch to diesel haulage for the final stage. However, a downturn in coal trade and a need to replace the ageing Class 76 locomotives led to the trans-Pennine route's closure east of Hadfield, with the last train running on July 17, 1981. Hopes of reopening the line quickly ended when most of the line east of Hadfield was lifted in the mid-1980s, but there are still regular calls for the powers-that-be to have second thoughts, despite the conversion of part of the trackbed to a cyclepath.

In October 1973, members of Organisation of the Petroleum Exporting Countries (OPEC) declared an oil embargo in response to the decision of the USA to resupply the Israeli army during the Yom Kippur war.

Provoking fuel shortages in Britain, just as the 2011 Libyan crisis has seen the price of fuel at the pumps soar, the embargo lasted until March 1974, but by then had showed that it was folly to rely on road transport alone, and what was needed was an energy efficient and adequate public transport network.

One of the last Beeching closures was the GWR branch from Maiden Newton on the main line to Weymouth and Bridport.

Initially closure had been staved off because the narrow roads of the locality prompted a subsidy from Dorset County Council. However, the final trains ran in May 1975.

In the north of England, the Haltwhistle-Alston branch in the Pennines had survived Beeching's closure recommendation because of the lack of an all-weather road as an alternative. It lingered on until May 3, 1976 with the last train running two days earlier.

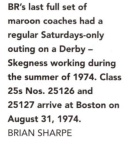

BR's last full set of maroon coaches had a regular Saturdays-only outing on a Derby – Skegness working during the summer of 1974. Class 25s Nos. 25126 and 25127 arrive at Boston on August 31, 1974.
BRIAN SHARPE

The last day of British Rail services at Tunbridge Wells West on July 6, 1985. It was the last British Rail line to close to passengers. PHIL BARNES

Above: **Class 76 No. 76001 heads towards Woodhead with a freight at Torside on October 28, 1975. The Woodhead route is now no more.**
BRIAN SHARPE

Left: **No. 76037 heads a short freight past Torside on October 28, 1975**
BRIAN SHARPE

Beeching: 55 Years of the Axe Man **101**

Birmingham Snow Hill station saw its last trains to Wolverhampton via Smethwick withdrawn on March 6, 1972. The Great Western Hotel at the front had been demolished in 1969, and afterwards the derelict station became a car park, until most of it was knocked down in 1977. MIKE ESAU

The UK railway network showing the lines closed in red, and the existing lines in the late 20th century in black. NRM

By the mid-seventies, with the last of the Beeching closure out of the way, the network had shrunk to 12,000 miles of track and 2000 stations, around the same size it is now.

One Beeching closure was not enacted until 1985. It was the line from Eridge to Tunbridge Wells, which had been earmarked for the axe along with services from Brighton to Tonbridge.

Tunbridge Wells West station was itself listed for closure in 1966, but subsequently reprieved. However, services on the line were restricted to shuttles between Tonbridge and Eridge with a few through trains to Uckfield.

By the early 1980s the track and signalling needed to be replaced. British Rail decided that the cost of keeping the line from Eridge to Tunbridge Wells Central station open by Grove Junction did not justify the cost of £175,000. Despite public objections, the line closed from July 6, 1985. It was believed though that Tunbridge Wells West station was the last on British Rail to have gas lighting.

A serpent from Serpell

Apart from the years 1978-80, when passenger numbers grew in successive years, the overall decline which had begun in 1957 continued.

Rock bottom was reached in 1982 with the lowest number of passenger journeys of the second half of the 20th century, possibly as a result of a rail strike over rostering arrangements, the lowest level of passenger miles, and the lowest level of passenger revenue since 1968.

Revenue had decreased steadily from £2300 million in 1970 to £1800 million in 1982, while costs had risen from £2500 million to £2700 million. The passenger deficit was £933 million.

Meanwhile, car ownership was at an all-time high and continuing to soar year by year.

It was probably inevitable that a Conservative Government headed by Margaret Thatcher which was marked by a drive towards self sufficiently would re-examine the rail network sooner than later.

That year, one was indeed commissioned, and produced by a committee chaired by Sir David Serpell KCB CMG OBE, a senior civil servant who had worked under none other than Dr Beeching. However, even by the standards of the junked Beeching Mark 2 report of 1965, its recommendations began at 'brutal' and got worse.

In short, the Serpell Report, correctly named Railway Finances, offered the option of reducing the 10,370 route miles of the UK network down to a skeletal network of just 1630 miles.

The bulk of the report, published in January 1983, examined in depth the state of British Rail's finances in 1982, while its second part considered a series of options and variations of them for the network as it might appear in 1992.

The first option would be to aim for a commercial network, in which the railways as a whole would make a profit. To do that, route mileage would have to be cut by a staggering 84%t, and annual passenger miles by 56%. That would leave London-Bristol/Cardiff, London-Birmingham-Liverpool/Manchester-Glasgow/Edinburgh, and London-Leeds/Newcastle as the only main line left.

This plan would keep some of the London commuter lines in the Home Counties, but all others would close.

The loss-making passenger sector would be subsidised by profits from the freight sector.

The second option was almost identical to the first, apart for making provision for the cost of tackling road congestion caused by rail closures. If the overall cost to the nation of closing a railway line was greater than saving it once road congestion had been considered, it would be kept. This second option would still cut route mileage by 78%, and annual passenger miles by 45%, keeping most of the London commuter lines.

The third option took a different tack, by offering various ways to cut the annual deficit through specific targets. One of these would have kept the existing network virtually intact, apart from the worst of the loss-making routes and closing many smaller stations. Listed among the 1% of the network that would close here was the Westbury-Weymouth line. Overall passenger miles would have been cut by only 4%.

Another target suggested was to cut the annual deficit to £700 million, by closing more loss-making services such as the Tarka Line from Exeter to Barnstaple, Trowbridge-Melksham-Chippenham line, the Norwich to Cromer and Sheringham branch, the Central Wales Line and the Cambrian Coast Main Line west of Shrewsbury.

An ever harsher target would be to reduce the deficit to $500 million a year. That would have seen the elimination of all lines in East Anglia apart from the line to Norwich, all routes in Wales apart from the valley lines north of Cardiff, all rural routes in Scotland, all lines in Devon and Cornwall other than the GWR main line to Exeter; the Salisbury-Exeter line, the trans-Pennine line; and most local routes east of the East Coast Main Line. This would have slashed route mileage by 39%, and yearly passenger miles reduced by 15%.

A fourth option would dispense with the overriding financial restraint, and keep routes serving communities with a population greater than 25,000.

The Serpell Report was immediately pounced on by rail supporters, who said that it did not consider improvements to rail services as a means of attracting passengers. It was labelled as a 'second Beeching' because of its focus on closing secondary routes.

Matters were made worse by the fact that Transport Minister David Howell, who had commissioned the report, sat on it for a month after receiving it, during which time parts were leaked to the press, generating anger and fears among commuters and the rail unions.

The government blamed British Rail for the leaks, which a grateful Labour party under Michael Foot made much of. With a general election looming, many Conservative MPs became nervous.

The popular British Rail chairman from 1976-83 Sir Peter Parker said that he found Serpell "as cosy as a razor blade". He exploited the report's suggested closures to persuade the train drivers' union ASLEF to call off a threatened strike that would have shut the rail system. Serpell, then 70, who had become permanent secretary at the Ministry of Transport in 1968, even endured personal abuse from a guard on his train home to Devon.

Largely because of the report's extremely harsh first option, it met with so much fierce resistance from many quarters that it was quickly abandoned, and there were no changes to the network made. However, it nonetheless reflected the way in which some in high places were thinking, and pre-empted the following years, in which British Rail was often accused by the unions of trying to cut costs and close lines by introducing 'Serpell by stealth'. The Serpell Report led to the end of Howell's ministerial career, many believed, for after the Conservatives' crushing victory in the April 1983 election, Thatcher dropped him from the cabinet.

However, passenger numbers improved through the mid and late Eighties, reaching a 20-year high in 1988, and with privatisation on the horizon in 1993, the Serpell Report was consigned to history.

Serpell decided to retire for good, and moved to Dartmouth, ironically the only town in Britain with a station that famously has never had a railway running into it, for it was built on the opposite side of the river from the rail terminus at Kingswear, to which it was linked by ferry. He died on July 28, 2008 at the aged of 96.

How Britain's railway network would have looked had the Serpell Report of 1982 been implemented.

The terminus of the Bridport branch in 1963, earmarked for the Beeching Axe, it took until 1975 for it to close. BEN BROOKSBANK/CREATIVE COMMONS

Chapter Twelve

Great Beeching *survivors*

While banner-waving protestors who gathered outside stations on the last day of services on their local line may have felt that they were wasting their breath against a Government 'one size fits all' policy, that the consultation procedures were purely academic, and that the Labour government which pledged to reverse the cuts re-engaged on that promise after it won two general elections in 1964, several lines were reprieved sooner or later.

On March 3, 1964, nearly a year after the publication of the Beeching report, Marples announced that he had refused consent to closure in two cases – the Central Wales Line between Craven Arms, Pontardulais and Llanelli (now marketed as the Heart of Wales Line), and the Ayr-Kilmarnock line in Scotland. He did, however, agree to the closure of the southernmost branch of the Central Wales Line between Pontardulais and Swansea Victoria, from June that year.

Regarding the Central Wales Line, Marples said he had taken on board the fact that it served several towns and villages in central Wales, some of which had no other public transport and few of which had even a daily bus; it also provided a cross-country link between Swansea, west Wales and the north of England. He did accept that some stations and halts were all but unused and told the British Railways Board that he would be prepared to consider their closure.

Regarding Ayr-Kilmarnock, Marples endorsed the finding of the Scottish Transport Users Consultative Committee, but said he might reconsider in another 12 months.

Marples said that the railways' annual operating loss had been reduced by about £17 million in 1963, and that progress was being made, but un-remunerative passenger services listed by Beeching were costing the taxpayer at least £30 million in annual subsidies, a heavy burden which had to be reduced.

Marples said: "That is far from being the case. Most of my consents are not just 'yes', they are 'yes, but…'".

Some of his consents had no conditions except maintenance of existing bus services; others were consents with special requirements for extra bus services; others were consents deferred to give time for road improvements; and yet others were consents with the proviso that warning must be given if British Railways wished to take up the track.

104 Beeching: 55 Years of the Axe Man

Marples said that he was taking into account all important factors, including social considerations, the pattern of industrial development and possible effects on roads and road traffic. "They also show that in every case, I have accepted the Transport Users Consultative Committee's view on hardship almost entirely," he said. "This shows how much I rely on them. I have also nearly always accepted their proposals for extra services to relieve hardship, and sometimes I have gone further than they recommended.

"We look at everything that has a bearing on each proposal – buses, roads, traffic, regional development, commuting needs, holiday travel. All the facts are brought to an official working party, on which all Government departments with relevant responsibilities are represented. They report to me, and I consider each case personally."

Marples decision on the Central Wales Line came despite observations made by the Transport Users Consultative Committee that between Llandovery and Craven Arms, only the stations at Knighton and Llandrindod Wells were taking more than £5 a day in receipts. Yet the TUCC also said that the withdrawal of services would cause considerable hardship.

Nevertheless, the line was reduced to single track during 1964/5 as an economy measure.

A second closure threat appeared in 1967, but the line again reprieved, on social grounds.

Sceptics said that Harold Wilson saved it from closure because it passed through six marginal constituencies.

British Rail continued to seek economies despite receiving a subsidy to operate the line, and in 1972, produced a stroke of inspiration, one which might have saved many other lines in the Beeching report. It successfully applied for a Light Railway Order under the 1896 Act for the section of the 78¾ mile section of the line between Craven Arms and Pantyffynnon, even though the line speed is 60mph and not the required 25mph. However, the order still allowed many operational procedures to be simplified and so produced economies.

The future of the line was again thrown into question in 1987 when the Glanrhyd bridge near Llandeilo collapsed after heavy flooding, and an early morning northbound diesel multiple unit plunged into the swollen River Towy, killing four people. The Carmarthen-Aberystwyth line had been closed in 1965 following serious flood damage because the cost of repairs was deemed uneconomic, but in the case of the Central Wales Line, by then there was unanimous support for the line to be saved.

The Central Wales Line is one of the greatest of all Beeching survivors. Preserved BR Standard 4MT 2-6-4T No. 80079 and LMS 'Black Five' No. 44767 *George Stephenson* are seen heading a charter into Sugar Loaf tunnel on June 6, 1993.
BRIAN SHARPE

It could so easily be the Beeching era rather than the 21st century: LMS Stanier 8F No. 48151 heads a rake of maroon coaches on the Far North Line between Inverness and Thurso and Wick. BRIAN SHARPE

Marples refused to save the Caernarfon to Afon Wen branch. The isolated signalbox at Penygroes station is pictured after closure. MIKE ESAU

Marples again saved the day

In spring 1964, Ernest Marples announced a reprieve for the heavily lossmaking routes tot he north and West of Inverness, the Far North Line to Wick and Thurso and the Kyle of Lochalsh branch.

If Beeching's recommendations had been adopted, there would have been no trains north of Stirling.

However, after listening to the powerful Highland lobby, the transport minister agreed that that transport in the region was a special case. At the time there was no realistic prospect of alternative road transport to replace it, and the line closures could cause extreme and widespread hardship for the sake of saving £360,000 a year.

Conversely, British Railways then promised to make the services more attractive to promote greater use by both passengers and freight.

The Kyle line appeared at risk again in the Seventies when the Stornaway ferry was switched to Ullapool, but tourism and again social considerations saved the day.

In September 1964, Ernest Marples sanctioned the closure of 38 passenger routes, as recommended by Beeching, but reprieved three others. These were Newcastle-Riverside-Tynemouth, the previous mentioned Middlesbrough-Whitby, and Llandudno Junction-Blaenau Ffestiniog.

He also redeemed two others, the Darlington-Bishop Auckland section of the Darlington-Crook line, along with the Bangor-Caernarfon section of the Bangor-Afon Wen route.

He stopped the closure of Newcastle-Tynemouth because it carried large numbers of workers to and from the Tyne shipyards in a badly-congested area. The Tyne & Wear Metro light rail system now links the two.

In the case of the 28 mile wonderfully-scenic Blaenau Ffestiniog line, he was swayed by both by the hardship which closure would cause to local residents, particularly

Preserved LMS 'Black Five' 4-6-0 No. 45407 pulls into Kyle of Lochalsh station with the 'North Briton' railtour on August 5, 2006. Beeching recommended this beautiful line for closure, but today mainland ports for the Isle of Skye are served by two rail lines, the other being the West Highland extension from Fort William to Mallaig which has also warded off closure threats. BRIAN SHARPE

in winter when the road to Blaenau over the Crimea Pass is affected by snow and ice, and also by tourism.

Nonetheless, he agreed to the closure of the stations at Glan Conwy and Dolgarrog.

From 1964, the line was used for nuclear flask traffic to Trawsfynydd power station. The GWR route from Blaenau to Bala which closed in 1961 after being flooded by Llyn Celyn reservoir was partially reopened in 1964 from Blaenau to Trawsfynydd, with a new rail connection built to link it at Blaenau to the line to Llandudno Junction. Power station traffic ceased in 1998 and that part of the line is now mothballed.

The Blaenau branch is now marketed as the Conwy Valley Line, and in 1982, opened a new interchange station with the Ffestiniog Railway in the town. Glan Conwy and Dolgarrog have since been reopened.

Sadly, while the magnificent Conwy Valley line was reprieved, around the same time another spectacular route, the 53 mile GWR line between Ruabon and Morfa Mawddach via Bala was closed. Two sections have been reopened as heritage lines; Llangollen-Carrog (Corwen scheduled for 2012) as the standard gauge Llangollen Railway, and the length along the shores of Llyn Tegid (Lake Bala) as the 1ft 11½in gauge Bala Lake Railway.

The service between Bishop Auckland and Darlington was retained for use by large numbers of workers from Bishop Auckland travelling to work in the Darlington-Aycliffe 'Growth Area'. Bishop Auckland was seen as a railhead for the Crook-Tow Law region.

It not only survives today, but links to the Weardale Railway, a largely pre-Beeching passenger closure which has been revived for passenger and freight services by US operator British American Rail Services.

The Bangor-Caernarfon line was spared because Marples accepted that it provided a much better railhead than Bangor for travellers via the North Wales Coast Line to and from places farther south, including Pwllheli and the Butlin's holiday camp at Penychain. However, his successors did not share the same view.

It was closed to passenger traffic on January 5, 1970. Following the fire that severely damaged the railway bridge over the Menai Strait, the branch and Caernarfon goods yard were temporarily reopened for goods traffic from May 23, 1970 to January 30 1972. Following closure all the track was removed and the station was demolished.

Caernarfon had a new station opened on 11 October 1997, but with a line running south along the trackbed of the Afon Wen route for which Marples had sanctioned closure when reprieving Bangor-Caernarfon.

It was the first part of a new Welsh Highland Railway which was being developed by the Ffestiniog Railway and which included the route of its predecessor that had closed on September 5, 1936. The completed and extended new Welsh Highland saw its first public services through to Porthmadog on February 19, 2011, and as that town has a main line station, Caernarfon can now be said to have been reconnected by rail to the national network.

The stations at Delphinine and Carr Bridge on the Perth-Inverness line were saved because they serve isolated communities largely dependent on the tourist trade, and are still open today.

Marples took the view that it would be extremely expensive to provide adequate alternative services. However, it still remains the fact that under both him and his Labour successors, far many more lines and stations to which closure objections had been raised were axed.

With the town's giant trademark slate waste heaps as a background, double Fairlie *Earl of Merioneth* steams out of Blaenau Ffestiniog station at the head of the 1.40pm to Porthmadog on September 19, 2009, with Western Region diesel hydraulic D1015 *Western Champion*, in its early Sixties Beeching era golden ochre livery, and heading Pathfinder Tours 'Western Slater' main line outing from Didcot stabled with its train in the Conwy Valley Line run-round loop. ROGER DIMMICK/FR

Anti-closure campaigner Graham Nuttall with his faithful companion Ruswarp, and the petition signed by 32,000 people and the border collie. Although they saved the day for one of Britain's most beautiful railway routes, their story was to end in tragedy.

The pair travelled by train from Burnley to Llandrindod Wells on January 20, 1990 to go walking in the mountains. Neighbours raised the alarm after they failed to return, but despite exhaustive searches along with missing person posters and leaflets, there was no news.

Finally, on April 7, walker David Clarke found the body of 41-year-old Graham by a mountain stream. Next to him was Ruswarp, 14, who had stood guard over his master through snow and rain. Ruswarp had become so weak that he had to be carried off the mountain, and despite vetinary treatment he died shortly after attending his master's funeral.
FRIENDS OF THE SETTLE-CARLISLE LINE

A bronze statue of Ruswarp was unveiled at Garsdale station in 2009. Mark Rand, chairman of the Friends of the Settle to Carlisle Line, said that the statue not only symbolised the successful fight to save the line but also the loyalty of man's best friend. CHRIS DIXON

Settle and Carlisle

Following the closure of smaller intermediate stations in the 1960s, the Beeching report recommended the withdrawal of all passenger services from one of Britain's most scenic and best-loved routes, the Settle to Carlisle line.

The Beeching recommendations were shelved, but in May 1970 all stations apart from Settle and Appleby West were closed, and local passenger services cut to two trains a day in each direction, leaving mostly freight.

The 'Thames-Clyde Express' from London to Glasgow Central via Leicester was withdrawn in 1975, and night sleepers from London to Glasgow using the route followed the year afterwards. A residual service from Glasgow to Nottingham survived until May 1982.

It was clear that the line and its viaducts and tunnels were suffering from lack of investment, and deterioration might yet do the job of the Beeching Axe. During the 1970s, most freight traffic was diverted onto the electrified West Coast Main Line. As a counter measure, Dalesrail began operating services to closed stations on summer weekends in 1974, promoted by the Yorkshire Dales National Park Authority to encourage ramblers.

Yet by the early 1980s, the route handled only a handful of trains per day, and there were those who head the cogwheels turning in British Rail's mind from afar. In 1981 a protest group, the Friends of the Settle-Carlisle Line was set up to campaign against the line's closure even before it was officially announced.

Between 1983 and 1984 three closure notices were posted up by British Rail which was determined to shut the route. While the Beeching threat had been staved off, this time BR saw no need for the line which had lost its freight, through passenger services and had a very limited local service. BR also considered Ribblehead Viaduct to be in an unsafe condition, and used it as the key reason for closure, stating that its repair or replacement could cost more than £6 million.

Above: **Irony here as A1 Peppercorn Pacific No 60163 *Tornado*, a new example of the class which was rendered extinct during the scramble to dieselise in the Sixties, heads through Ribblehead station, which was closed by Beeching and later reopened, the Settle & Carlisle line being reprieved in 1989.** BRIAN SHARPE

Freight ended in 1983, although more enthusiast steam specials were by then running over it.

As the threat of closure hung over the line, passenger use underwent a resurgence, as packed Class 47-hauled trains carried people wanting to travel the line for one last time. Annual journeys were recorded at 93,000 in 1983 when the campaign against closure began, and had shot up to 450,000 by 1989.

Plans were even drawn up in 1987 to sell the line off to a private bidder. However, 22,000 signed a petition against closure, and eventually, on April 11, 1989, the recently-promoted Conservative Transport Minister Paul Channon announced that the closure notices had been withdrawn. In 1991, work began on repairing Ribblehead viaduct.

The decision was the right one. While it may be easy to justify closing a line because of the current viability, how often are future traffic flows predicted, or how far can they be expected to be foreseen?

Much freight now uses the Settle and Carlisle route due to congestion on the West Coast Main Line, and includes coal from the Hunterston coal terminal in Scotland taken to power stations in Yorkshire, and gypsum from Drax Power Station carried to Kirkby Thore. Significant engineering work was needed to upgrade the line to carry such heavy freight traffic and additional investment made to reduce the length of signal sections.

The line is also used as a diversionary route from the West Coast Main Line during engineering works, while eight of the stations closed in 1970 were reopened.

In 2009 a bronze statue of Ruswarp, a collie dog belonging to Graham Nuttall, the first secretary of the Friends of the Settle-Carlisle Line, was unveiled on the platform of the refurbished Garsdale station. It is there to mark the saving of the line by people power, and the fact that Ruswarp is believed to be the only dog to sign a petition against a rail closure originally proposed by Beeching, or any other for that matter.

Left: **A pair of EWS Class 37 diesels top and tail a train through Ribblehead station on the reprieved Settle & Carlisle line. Some of the anti-closure campaigners were so enthused by their victory that they formed a group to revive the Wensleydale line from Northallerton to Redmire and eventually Hawes, a pre-Beeching passenger closure.** BRIAN SHARPE

The famous *Jolly Fisherman* poster which promoted rail travel to Skegness on a branch which Beeching wanted to close. NRM

One of the great anomalies both of the development of the railway network in Victorian times and subsequent settlement patterns, and the Beeching closures is that while towns like Dudley (population 194,000), Blithe (36,000), Rushden/Higham Ferrers (35,500), Peterlee (30,000) and Coalville (30,000) no longer have a railway station, a tiny halt like Hubberts Bridge on the Grantham-Skegness line which serves only a handful of houses is still very much open. ROBIN JONES

A fisherman still jolly

In October 1960, Mablethorpe & Sutton Urban District Council voiced concerns when British Railways announced its intention to close the route from Louth to Mablethorpe, the northern part of a loop serving the resort popular with East Midlands and northern families.

As most of the holiday traffic to Mablethorpe and Sutton came over the southern half of the loop via Willoughby, closure of the Louth line was seen as having little impact.

There was little opposition to the closure and the last trains ran on December 3, 1960.

Yet while the British Transport Commission said that the remaining services to Mablethorpe from the south would remain, with improved stabling facilities at the resort to facilitate an increased number of excursion trains, councillors remained fearful that within a few years that line would close too.

They were right: British Railways failed to honour pledges to develop holiday traffic to Mablethorpe and Sutton, instead reducing both services and the availability of cheap tickets. For them, it was no surprise that the Beeching report of 1963 proposed the closure of virtually the whole of the East Lincolnshire network.

Lined up for the axe was the original Great Northern railway main line from Grimsby to London via Boston and Peterborough, Lincoln–Firsby via Bardney, Willoughby-Mablethorpe and the Skegness branch.

It was the railway that had turned Skegness from a tiny village into a massive resort. The Great Northern Railway's Jolly Fisherman poster extolling the virtues of the windswept North Sea coastal town because it was so

110 Beeching: 55 Years of the Axe Man

It seems incredible that there is no direct route today from Boston to Peterborough and on to London without going the 'long way round' via Sleaford. The station building at Sutterton is now a commercial premises. ROBIN JONES

The former stationmaster's house at Sutton-on-Sea is now a private residence.

The East Suffolk Line, a secondary coastal route between Ipswich and Lowestoft, was also earmarked for closure but reprieved by Barbara Castle in 1966 after a public inquiry, although its Beccles to Great Yarmouth section had been axed in 1958. The Minister declined to save the Saxmundham to Aldeburgh branch which closed on September 12, 1966. However, the line was singled in many places in 1984, and through services to London were withdrawn. Preserved Britannia Pacific No. 70013 *Oliver Cromwell* is seen crossing the swing bridge at Oulton Broad. BRIAN SHARPE

A unique survivor among the Beeching cuts is a 13¾ mile section of the Nottingham Midland to Melton Mowbray line, which was part of the Midland Railway's through route from Kettering to Nottingham.

After the line closed to passengers on June 6, 1966, and the through route from 1968, it was acquired by the British Rail Research Department at Derby and converted into an electrified test track for new trains initially for the Advanced Passenger Train project and in recent times the Virgin Trains Class 390 Pendolino units, London Underground trains and Bombardier's London Overground two-car class 172/0 DMU.

The Old Dalby test track the only proper one of its kind in Britain today, is now owned by BRB (Residuary) Ltd, the property-owning surviving remnant of British Rail following privatisation of 1993.

The pictured intermediate station at Widmerpool was built a mile-and-a-half from the small village it purported to serve, and was closed to passengers as early as 1949.

The main station building was converted into a pub and restaurant just before the line closed. It was originally called the Schooner Inn and later the Pullman Inn.
ROBIN JONES

bracing became one of the most famous and successful pieces of railway advertising of all time.

Freight traffic over the Mablethorpe line was withdrawn from March 30, 1964 but opposition to the loss of the passenger services was long and bitter, with a public hearing being held in Skegness on September 15/16, 1964. By the time the hearing took place, in the case of the rundown Mablethorpe branch, British Railways was able to argue that fewer passengers were likely to suffer hardship because by then, local residents had been deterred from using the services by the reductions.

Mablethorpe and Sutton Urban District Council wanted the line to stay because it said that roads from the proposed railhead at Boston were poor or inadequate. The Minister of Transport studied the findings of the inquiry and ordered British Railways to reconsider the closure plans. It did so, and proposed the same closures, but saving the Boston to Skegness line.

A second Transport Users Consultative Committee inquiry was held at Skegness in May 1968 and this time the transport minister backed the requested closures. He said that while closing the Mablethorpe line would affect the summer tourist trade, as at numerous resorts elsewhere in Britain, there were not enough users of the service during the rest of the year to justify keeping the service.

The Mablethorpe line closed from October 5, 1970 and was lifted the following year. Skegness and Boston remain linked to the national network via the route to Sleaford, Grantham and Nottingham, now rebranded and promoted as the Poacher Line. The mass influx of summer seaside specials is now consigned to history, but the Jolly Fisherman remains as the trademark of Skegness.

Chapter Thirteen

Reopenings
as heritage railways

Four years after leaving British Railways, Dr Beeching was back – to reopen the line to Buckfastleigh which closed before his time, as the preserved Dart Valley Railway. JOHN BRODRIBB

Back in 1962, as we saw earlier, Dr Beeching opened a new station on the Bluebell Railway, which was the first section of the British Railways main line network to be closed and then reopened as a private venture by volunteers and enthusiasts. Today, such heritage railways account for a major slice of Britain's tourist industry.

From such small beginnings, there are 108 operating railways and 60 more steam centres in the British Isles. Laid end to end, they would total more than 500 miles with 399 stations, a greater route mileage than that of the London Underground system and longer than the distance between London and Glasgow. More heritage railways are planned.

By the end of the 'noughties', heritage railways and museums carried 6.7 million passengers and earned around £81 million. They directly employ around 2000 people and are backed up by an army of nearly 18,000 volunteers and many, many more armchair supporters.

Many of them run over routes that Beeching closed, and yet are showing an operating profit, which his almost always ploughed back into infrastructure, or breaking even.

Therefore, does this not show that Beeching got his sums wrong?

By no means – in fact, quite the opposite.

When many branch lines were axed in the early Sixties, often communities which had rallied round in vain to try to save them subsequently looked at taking them over by themselves. A classic example is the Keighley & Worth Valley Railway, where the entire five-mile branch from Keighley to Oxenhope was saved by the local community and after reopening in 1968, went on to worldwide fame as the setting for the EMI film of Edith A Nesbit's children's classic The Railway Children.

Yet how many of them ever managed to run conventional daily public services round the year, as opposed to seasonal tourist lines showcasing restored heritage steam and diesel locomotives and rolling stock?

The answer is not many. Not even a handful.

On April 5, 1969, after the Dart Valley Railway bought the line from British Rail, the first preservation era trains ran over the Ashburton branch in Devon from Buckfastleigh to a point near the main line junction north of Totnes, under the new operator's Light Railway Order, with GWR pannier tank No. 6412.

This heritage line was officially opened by none other than 'axeman' Dr Richard Beeching himself – even though it was not one of the many branches that he had infamously closed.

However, in another twist to the battle between road and rail, the revivalists failed to persuade the Ministry of Transport not to take the top portion of the route, the two-mile stretch from Buckfastleigh to Ashburton, for use as part of the new A38 dual carriageway trunk road from Exeter to Plymouth, and therefore the entire branch was not saved, as had been the case with the KWVR.

The year before, British Rail had announced its intention to close the seven-mile Paignton to Kingswear section of the branch from Newton Abbot, in many ways a main line in all but name.

Many eyebrows were raised when the Dart Valley Railway successfully bid to buy it, taking it over from British Rail in service, without any 'last day' trains and the like associated with the Beeching closures.

The line was bought as a going concern on January 30, 1972, the purchase price being $250,000 with a further $25,000 paid for signalling alterations at Paignton. Most of this was recouped from the sale of the Royal Dart Hotel at Kingswear and other surplus land.

A new independent station was built at Paignton Queen's Park alongside the British Rail station to serve the Kingswear trains and a winter service was run from 1 January 1973.

However, the operating figures did not stack up for either British Rail or the new owners. It quickly became clear that the Dart Valley Railway could not afford to run a daily service round the year, and so from the end of summer 1973 it became a purely seasonal operation.

Dart Valley Railway plc found that the glorious coastal scenery reaped big dividends, while as the years wore on, the original Buckfastleigh line incurred losses. To cut a very long story short, the Buckfastleigh line was eventually sold to the line's volunteer supporters association, which had rebranded it as the South Devon Railway, and thanks to freely-given labour, very much flourishes today. Meanwhile, the Paignton-Kingswear line, now branded the Dartmouth Steam railway and River Boat Company, is the only heritage line in Britain to pay annual dividends to its shareholders, relying on paid staff and having built up a transport empire including a boat fleet.

A revived line earmarked for closure for Beeching was the Minehead branch, known today as the West Somerset Railway, reopened in stages between Minehead and the first original station on the branch proper, Bishops Lydeard, between 1976-79, it tried to run regular services for local people, using classic diesel multiple units painted in 1950s carmine and cream livery. The figures also did not stack up here, and the line was hampered by not being allowed to run over the main line into Taunton, as did the branch trains under the GWR and British Railways.

The world's most famous steam locomotive, LNER A3 Pacific No. 4472 *Flying Scotsman*, steams over Broadsands viaduct between Paignton and Dartmouth on September 1, 1973.
BRIAN SHARPE

GWR 2-8-0 No 3803, on loan from the South Devon Railway, departs from Toddington on the Gloucestershire Warwickshire Railway. Father's Day, June 2010.
ROBIN JONES

Beeching: 55 Years of the Axe Man 113

While the Beeching closure of the Great Central Railway's London Extension, which had been built to continental loading gauge and therefore able to handle Channel Tunnel traffic, may be considered as a loss to the country, it has been the heritage sector's gain. Three sections are preserved – the Great Central Railway from Loughborough to Leicester North, the separate Great Central Railway (Nottingham) from Loughborough to Ruddington and the Buckinghamshire Railway Centre at Quainton Road station. The GCR is the world's only double-track heritage trunk line and can be used to recreate scenarios from the past. Original Great Central Robinson O4 2-8-0 No. 63601 approached Kinchley Lane with a demonstration mixed freight train. ROBIN JONES

Although the main line connection at Norton Fitzwarren still existed, one reason given in the early Eighties was that it would make a connecting bus service between Taunton and Bishops Lydeard obsolete, and unions would object to its driver being made redundant.

Other heritage lines will argue that they have provided 'real' public transport as opposed to tourist or heritage trains. The 15in gauge Romney Hythe & Dymchurch Railway, long billed as a main line in miniature, has run regular school trains for local youngsters. The Swanage Railway, which managed to rebuild half the London & South Western Railway branch line from the resort westwards, was hailed as a huge success because of the park-and-ride facility at its eastern terminus of Norden was credited with easing summer congestion on the A351, the spine road of the Isle of Purbeck.

Yet the reality is that none of them have replicated the services that ended under Beeching and British Railways, despite the provision of volunteer labour to maintain both rolling stock and infrastructure. What has been produced by preservationists is magnificent beyond belief, giving new generations an insight into the glory days of Britain's railway past and the chance to ride behind steam engines once again polished to perfection, but each of them is a very different animal to the running of a regular public timetable service 362 days a year.

If, of course, a local authority was to step in and subsidise commuter or shopper services on these lines, it would be a different matter indeed. With fears of global fuel shortages – such as that of 2011– and a growing desire to conserve the environment and avoid traffic congestion, fresh new opportunities may well arise here.

Yet how far has any heritage railway revival scheme proved Beeching wrong?

If it were possible to run seaside branch lines only during the summer season, many more could have been

Several lines closed by Dr Beeching have been revived as narrow gauge tourist railways. Who would have guessed from this 2008 view of Quarry Hunslet 0-4-0 saddle tank *Lilian* that the Launceston Steam railway lies on the route of the fabled 'Atlantic Coast Express' which ran from Waterloo to Padstow until the Sixties? JONATHAN MANN/LSR

saved, but Beeching would be quick to point out the enormous cost of storing and maintaining the rolling stock for the rest of the time when it would not be used, as well as that of maintaining the route infrastructure throughout the year. In any age where the car is king, such figures would never stack up.

LSWR T9 4-4-0 No. 30120 at Boscarne on the Bodmin & Wenford Railway, a revival Beeching closure, in September 2010.
ROBIN JONES

M7 tank engine No. 30479 pulls out of Alresford with the 11.12am Saturdays only train to Alton on September 3, 1955. The Alton-Winchester City line was recommended by closure by Beeching in 1963, but this did not happen for another 10 years. The Alton-Alresford section is now the Mid-Hants Railway.
HUGH BALLANTYNE

Ivatt MT 2-6-0 No. 46512 was relaunched into traffic on its Strathspey Railway home on March 11, 2011 following an overhaul. This heritage line runs from Aviemore to Broomhill on the line to Forres which lost its passenger services on October 18, 1965, and is hoping to rebuild the line eastwards to Boat of garden.
HENDY POLLOCK/ STRATHSPEY RAILWAY

Pre-Beeching passenger closures, now heritage lines

These lists refer to complete routes which were formerly run as part of the national network and which individual heritage lines mostly run over particular lengths.

- Battlefield Line: Nuneaton-Ashby: closed to passengers 1931, closed to goods 1970.
- Lynton & Barnstaple Railway closed 1935.
- Pontypool & Blaenavon Railway: closed to passengers 1941.
- Caledonian Railway (Brechin-Bridge of Dun): closed to passengers 1952.
- Bure Valley Railway (Aylsham-Wroxham section of County School-Wroxham: closed to passengers 1952.
- Weardale Railway (Bishop Auckland-Eastgate section of Bishop Auckland-Wearhead: closed to passengers 1953.
- Kent & East Sussex Railway: Headcorn to Robertsbridge closed to regular passenger trains 1954.
- Wensleydale Railway: Northallerton-Hawes closed to passengers 1954.
- Bo'ness & Kinneil Railway: closed to passengers 1956.
- Welshpool & Llanfair Light Railway closed 1956.
- Chinnor & Princes Risborough Railway: closed to passengers 1957.
- Bluebell Railway: East Grinstead-Lewes: closed to passengers 1958.
- South Devon Railway: Totnes-Ashburton: closed to passengers 1958.
- Cholsey & Wallingford Railway: closed to passengers 1959.
- Rudyard Lake Steam Railway: Leek-Macclesfield: closed to passengers 1960.
- Northampton & Lamport Railway: Northampton-Market Harborough closed to passengers 1960.
- Midland Railway-Butterley: Butterley-Ambergate-Mansfield closed to passengers 1961.
- Swindon & Cricklade Railway: Andover-Andoversford closed to passengers 1961.

Heritage railways on routes closed by Beeching

This list includes both routes contained in the 1963 Beeching report and those previously endorsed for closure during his first years as British Railways chairman.

- Avon Valley Railway: Mangotsfield – Bath Green Park closed to passengers 1966.
- Bala Lake Railway: Ruabon-Morfa Mawddach closed to passengers 1965.
- Berkeley Vale Railway: Berkeley Road-Sharpness closed to passengers 1964.
- Bluebell Railway: Haywards Heath-Ardingly-Horsted Keynes closed to passengers 1963.
- Buckinghamshire Railway Centre: Marylebone-Nottingham Victoria closed 1966.
- Bodmin & Wenford Railway: Bodmin Road-Padstow closed to passengers 1967.
- Brecon Mountain Railway: Newport-Dowlais-Brecon: closed to passengers 1962.
- Cambrian Railways: Gobowen-Oswestry closed to passengers 1966.
- Churnet Valley Railway: Leek-Uttoxeter closed to passengers 1965.
- Colne Valley Railway: Haverhill-Chappell & Wakes Colne closed to passengers 1961, freight 1965.
- Devon Railway Centre, Cadeleigh. Exeter – Dulverton line closed 1963
- East Anglian Railway Museum: Shelford – Marks Tey (but Sudbury to Marks Tey never closed).
- East Lancashire Railway: Manchester Victoria-Bury-Bacup closed to passengers 1966.
- East Somerset Railway: Witham-Yatton closed to

One line which fell victim to the Beeching Axe on March 7, 1966, when only 12 people turned up for the last train, was the Seaton branch, which ran alongside the River Axe. Its closure dealt a blow to the east Devon resort's seasonal trade. However, the branch was partially revived as the Seaton Tramway, a unique 2ft 9in gauge line that runs traditional street trams either cut down to two thirds of their original size, or built new to that scale.

Back in British Railways days, 1200 people used the branch on summer Saturdays, but that fell foul of the Beeching criteria that the storage of coaches for profitable peak-season operation of branch lines was grossly uneconomic. However, more than 100,000 visitors a year nowadays ride along the three-mile route between the original station building at Colyton and a new terminus at Seaton. A scheme to extend the tramway further towards the town centre has been mooted. However, no attempt has been made to extend the line further north along the rest of the old branch to Seaton Junction on the Waterloo-Exeter main line, a question frequently raised by visitors. SEATON TRAMWAY

passengers 1963.
- Embsay & Bolton Abbey Steam Railway Leeds City-Ilkley-Skipton closed to passengers 1965.
- Gartell Light Railway: Bath Green Park-Bournemouth West closed 1966.
- Great Central Railway and GCR (Marylebone-Nottingham Victoria closed as through route 1966, to local passenger services 1969.
- Gwili Railway: Carmarthen-Aberystwyth closed to passengers 1965.
- Helston Railway: Gwinear Road-Helston closed 1962.
- Isle of Wight Steam Railway: Ryde Pier Head-Ventnor/Cowes closed 1966.
- Keith & Dufftown Railway: Keith-Dufftown-Elgin closed to passengers 1965.
- Keighley & Worth Valley Railway: Keighley-Oxenhope closed 1962.
- Lappa Valley Railway: Newquay-Chacewater. Closed 1963.
- Lakeside & Haverthwaite Railway: Ulverston-Lakeside (Windermere) closed to passengers 1965.
- Launceston Steam Railway: Okehampton-Padstow closed to passengers 1966.
- Mid-Hants Railway Winchester City-Alton closed 1973.
- Lavender Line: Tunbridge Wells-Brighton-Uckfield-Lewes closed 1969.
- Lincolnshire Wolds Railway: Peterborough-Grimsby Town closed to passengers 1970.
- Llangollen Railway: Ruabon-Morfa Mawddach closed to passengers 1965.
- Nene Valley Railway: Rugby-Peterborough East closed to passengers 1966.
- North Norfolk Railway: Sheringham-Melton Constable closed 1964.
- North Yorkshire Moors Railway: Malton-Whitby closed 1965.
- Plym Valley Railway: Plymouth-Launceston: closed to passengers 1962.
- Severn Valley Railway: Bewdley-Shrewsbury closed to passengers 1963.
- South Tynedale Railway: Haltwhistle-Alston closed 1976
- Spa Valley Railway: Three Bridges-Tunbridge Wells West closed 1985.
- Strathspey Railway: Aviemore-Craigellachie/Forres closed to passengers 1965.
- Wells & Walsingham Railway: Dereham-Wells-next-the-Sea closed 1964.
- West Somerset Railway: Taunton-Minehead closed 1971.
- Welsh Highland Railway: Caernarfon to Dinas section, part of Caernarfon-Afon Wen, closed in December 1964.

Heritage lines on routes not proposed for closure by Beeching but subsequently closed

- Dartmoor Railway: Okehampton-Bere Alston: closed to passengers 1968, Exeter to Okehampton closed to passengers 1972.
- Dartmouth Steam Railway & River Boat Company: Paignton-Kingswear privatised in 1972.
- Gloucestershire Warwickshire Railway:
- Stratford-upon-Avon-Gloucester closed to passengers 1968.
- Mid-Norfolk Railway: Wymondham-Dereham: closed to passengers 1969.
- Peak Rail: Peak Forest Junction-Matlock closed 1968.
- Swanage Railway: Wareham-Swanage closed 1972.
- Vale of Rheidol Railway: Aberystwyth-Devil's Bridge sold by British Rail 1989.
- Wisbech & March Bramley line (not yet operational in 2011): closed in September 1968.

Great Northern Railway N2 0-6-2T No. 1744 departs from Keighley on the Keighley & Worth Valley Railway with GNR stock, February 2010.
BRIAN SHARPE

BR Standard 8P Pacific No. 71000 *Duke of Gloucester* heads away from Irwell Vale with a train for Rawtenstall on the East Lancashire Railway, October 2010.
BRIAN SHARPE

A moonlight flit to France

And what of Ernest Marples, the transport minister who, not Beeching, made the ultimate decision to close a third of Britain's railways?

Road builder Marples, who had spent his younger days working as a miner, a postman, a chef and an accountant, becoming an army captain during the Second World War , was elected to Parliament as conservative MP for Wallasey in 1945, and postmaster general in 1957, retired from the House of Commons at the February 1974 general election. Three months later, his public service was rewarded when he was made a life peer as Baron Marples of Wallasey.

In early 1975, before the end of the tax year, Marples fled without warning to the tax haven of Monaco, by the night ferry with his belongings packed into tea chests, after fighting off a reassessment of his financial assets.

It was said that he had formulated a plot to remove £2 million from Britain through his Liechtenstein company. He claimed he had been asked to pay unpaid tax dating back three decades.

After he had gone, discarded clothes and possessions were found scattered over the floors of his Belgravia home.

The late Fleet Street editor Richard Stott, when investigating Marples' flight to France, was told by him: "You are the worst journalist I have ever met. The most aggressive man I have ever met in my life."

The comment, of which Stott was immensely proud, was highlighted in the programme for the journalist's memorial service at St Clement Danes in the Strand on July 30, 2007 after he died at the age of 63.

The Government froze Marples' remaining assets in Britain for the next 10 years, but most of his fortune had by then been squirreled away to Monaco and Lichtenstein. He never returned to Britain, and spent the rest of his life in his French chateau at Fleurie, where he owned a vineyard, dying on July 6, 1978 in the Princess Grace Hospital Centre in Monaco.

It has since been claimed that when the late Lord Denning investigated the security aspects of the Profumo Affair in 1963, he told Prime Minister Harold Macmillan that a similar contemporary rumour, one concerning Marples, appeared to be true. Journalists claimed that the story was suppressed and was omitted from Denning's final report, but we will probably never know whether there is any truth in such claims.

GWR 0-6-0 pannier tank No. 6412 heads out of Wansford across the River Nene towards Peterborough during a loan visit to the Nene Valley Railway.
ROBIN JONES

LMS 'Jinty' 3F 0-6-0T No. 47279 departs from Stoneacre loop with a train from Bolton Abbey on the Embsay & Bolton Abbey Steam Railway. BRIAN SHARPE

Cadeleigh station on the Exe Valley line which was closed on October 7, 1963 is now the Devon Railway Centre, where a 2ft gauge line has been laid on part of the trackbed as a tourist attraction. In August 2010, three Kerr Stuart Wren class 0-4-0STs were seen in operation. ROBIN JONES

Chapter Fourteen

The unravelling *of the cuts*

Since the upsurge in rail traffic which began in the 1980s, and greater appreciation of the environmental damage caused by huge volumes of road traffic, both in terms of pollution and congestion, there has been a sea change towards railways.

The traditional tearing up of railway lines, often within days of them having closed, has ceased. At many locations around the country lie branch lines that are 'mothballed', the tracks intact, albeit heavily covered in vegetation.

One such example is the Anglesey Central Railway which runs from Gaerwen Junction on the Bangor-Holyhead line to Amlwch. It lost its passenger services to the Beeching Axe on December 5, 1964, with all stations closed, and goods yards, passing loops and sidings removed. However, the entire branch was saved to serve the Associated Octel bromine extraction plant at Amlwch.

In 1993, Octel's daily freight traffic was transferred to road haulage and all traffic on the Amlwch branch ended. The Octel plant closed in 2003, and has since been demolished, but the track remains in place. While local revivalists have sought to reopen it as a tourist line under the banner of Lein Amlwch, in 2011 the Welsh Assembly asked Network Rail to carry out a study into its possible reopening to serve the local community.

Similarly, the Trawsfynydd branch which served the nuclear power station in Snowdonia is still in place, 20 years after the complex closed down. There are periodic calls for it to be revived to carry tourists, but the key point is – it too has not been ripped up, as would have speedily been the case in the Sixties and Seventies. Scrapping a potential provider of 'green' transport is very much seen as politically incorrect in today's climate.

Who knows how many lines would have reopened by now if British Railways had adopted a similar approach then?

The extremely mothballed Amlwch branch near its terminus: back in the Sixties, such lines were often torn up within days of closure. But will it ever see trains again?
ROBIN JONES

Reversal successes

Since Dr Beeching produced his report in 1963, road traffic levels have grown significantly bringing gridlock to some areas. Housing developments of the Seventies and Eighties have turned small villages which in the days of steam barely justified a station or halt into thriving commuter settlements more than capable of justifying a rail connection.

At the same time, recent years have seen record levels of passengers on the railways. Around 1.2 billion passenger journeys in 2007/08, a rise of 45% on the figure from a decade earlier. There is also ever-increasing demand for more capacity on the network, and some of the Beeching cuts have been reversed.

Several closed stations have reopened, and passenger services been restored on lines where they had been withdrawn under the Sixties cuts. Many of them are in urban areas where the Passenger Transport Executives established by Barbara Castle's 1968 Transport Act have been tackling congestion by promoting rail use.

The prime example of the reversal of a Beeching closure in England is the Robin Hood Line between Nottingham and Worksop via Mansfield. Formed from two separate closed railways, it opened in stages between 1993-98.

Before then, Mansfield had been the largest town in Britain left without a rail link. It is one of the great idiosyncrasies of Victorian route planning combined with Beeching closures that towns like Mansfield and Leek can end up being disenfranchised from the national network, while you can still buy a ticket to delightful rural unstaffed halts such as Danzey for Tanworth or Wootton Wawen on the North Warwickshire Line.

Some reopenings took place fairly soon after closure. The section of the Lincoln to Peterborough line between Peterborough and Spalding closed to passengers on October 5, 1970 but reopened on June 7, 1971; Ruskington and Metheringham station reopened in October 1975.

The Great Western railway's Birmingham terminus of Snow Hill had been largely demolished, but a new replacement opened in 1987, along with the tunnel that ran south beneath the city centre to Moor Street and the old line to Kidderminster and Worcester. A new service between Birmingham and London, terminating at Marylebone rather than Paddington, was introduced.

The former line from Snow Hill running north to Wolverhampton has been reopened as part of the Midland Metro tram system. Several cities such as Manchester, Nottingham and Sheffield have built new modern light rail tram systems, some using old railway trackbeds in part.

Also in the West Midlands, the line from Coventry to Leamington was reopened on May 2, 1977, followed by the Coventry to Nuneaton line in 1988. A new station is to be provided at Kenilworth in 2013.

The Walsall-Hednesford line was reopened to passenger traffic in 1989 and extended to Rugeley in 1997. However, despite such successes, reopening has not been all plain sailing: the adjoining Walsall to Wolverhampton line saw its passenger trains withdrawn in 2008 on economic grounds.

In London, Snow Hill tunnel (not a Beeching closure) was reopened for passenger use in 1988, providing a link between the Midland Main Line from St Pancras and the

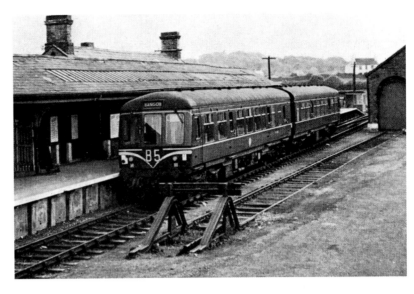

The 17¾ mile branch between Gaerwen Junction and Amlwch was closed from December 7, 1965. On June 2, 1961, a two-car diesel multiple unit prepared to leave Amlwch with the 7.12pm for Bangor.
ANDREW MUCKLEY/RM

The 1.50am auto train from Leamington Spa Avenue to Coventry restarts from Kenilworth on August 16, 1958 behind push-pull fitted Ivatt 2MT 2-6-2T No. 41228. Kenilworth station was closed in January 1965 along with the line, which was subsequently reopened minus this stop.
BRIAN MORRISON

Beeching: 55 Years of the Axe Man **121**

Beeching decimated the second and branch lines in the South Wales valleys. On March 13, 1964, three months before their last day, WR 0-6-0PT No. 9488 left Nelson & Llancaiach with the 3.55pm Pontypool Road-Swansea service, while on the left, GWR 0-6-2T No. 5634 has arrived with the 4.15pm Dowlais Cae Harris-Ystrad Mynach branch train. GERALD T ROBINSON/RM

network south of the River Thames via London Bridge station. Named Thameslink, it now offers a north-south cross-city rail link which also connects Bedford to Brighton.

Part of the Varsity Line closed in 1967 by the Wilson Government, the Oxford to Bicester Line was reopened in 1987 by the Network SouthEast sector of British Rail, and many believe that one day it will again be possible to catch a train from Oxford to Cambridge.

The London to Aylesbury line was extended north along the surviving freight-only part of the former Great Central main line to a new park-and-ride station called Aylesbury Vale Parkway which opened in December 2008.

Beeching had viewed South Wales as a declining industrial region, arguably with great clarity of vision in view of the pit closures which took place two decades later. His report led to the loss of most of the valleys network.

However, since 1983 the trend has been very much reversed, with four lines reopened within 20 miles – Abercynon-Aberdare, Barry-Bridgend via Llantwit Major, Bridgend-Maesteg and the Ebbw Valley branch via Newbridge, with 32 new stations opening.

While Scotland has repeatedly found itself at the forefront of closure threats, rail reopening south of the border have been something of a revelation.

Services on the Edinburgh-Bathgate line which reopened in 1986 now carry four times as many passengers as originally estimated. This enormous success led to the rebuilding and reopening of the 14 mile closed section between Airdrie and Bathgate in 2011.

Services on the Larkhall-Hamilton/Anniesland-Maryhill lines which reopened in 2005 have been carrying around 40% more passengers than previously predicted.

The Stirling-Alloa line was reopened on May 19, 2008 after a 40-year gap and was said to be carrying three times more passengers than estimated.

The northernmost 35 miles of the Waverley Route between Edinburgh and Galashiels via Dalkeith has been reopened with the backing of the Scottish Parliament.

Laurencekirk station on the main line between Aberdeen and Arbroath was shut in 1967 but reopened in May 2009, making it the 77th new or reopened station in Scotland since 1970. Across the country, more than 200 stations were reopened in the 1980s and early 90s, and in spite of the overall reduction in track and station capacity during the past 45 years since Beeching's cuts began bite hard, the network today carries around 30% more passengers than it did then. The Government expects that passenger numbers will increase by another 22% by 2014, with yet more growth in the following five years, as more people seek to avoid gridlock on urban roads, or choose to commute from further out.

In the mid Eighties, British Rail decided to reopen Birmingham Snow Hill station as part of a cross-city transport plan. In 1987, the newly-rebuilt station opened for services to the south, and services to London were restarted, but routed to Marylebone instead of the original GWR destination of Paddington. On September 24, 1995, services north to Smethwick and onwards to Worcester resumed, and in 1999, the GWR line to Wolverhampton was reopened as a light rail line, the Midland Metro, all of which indicated that its initial closure was short sighted. GMAN

Below: **Ebbw Vale Parkway on the reopened Ebbw Vale branch.**
ARRIVA TRAINS WALES

Could more lines reopen?

In 2009, Britain's Train Operating Companies issued a blueprint for reconnecting 40 stations on 14 routes to the national network at a cost of around £500 million, many having closed during the Beeching era, in order to improve access to rail for up to a million potential users.

Michael Roberts, chief executive of the Association of Train Operating Companies, said: "We have established that there is a strong business case for investment to bring a number of towns back on to the rail network.

"Now we need to safeguard these routes and develop the detailed case for investment."

A report by ATOC also calls for seven new park-and-ride stations, at Rushden (Northamptonshire), Peterlee (County Durham), Kenilworth (Warwickshire), Ilkeston and Clay Cross (Derbyshire), Ossett (West Yorkshire) and Wantage (Oxfordshire), to be built on existing lines and identified 20 more lines which could be reopening on employment grounds.

The report compiled by Chris Austin, ATOC former director of public policy, said the case for reopening more local stations and building 'parkways' has been boosted by lack of parking at main stations and congestion on roads leading to them.

The areas that would be served by the 14 lines identified in the report were:

- Aldridge and Brownhills in the West Midlands
- Ashington and Blyth in Northumberland
- Bordon, Hythe and Ringwood in Hampshire
- Brixham in Devon (served by a park-and-ride at nearby Churston on the Dartmouth Steam Railway rather than the original branch to the town)
- Cranleigh in Surrey
- Fleetwood, Rawtenstall and Skelmersdale in Lancashire
- Leicester to Burton in the East Midlands
- Wisbech in Cambridgeshire
- Washington in Tyne and Wear

Not all of the railways would need to be relaid: most of them were still served by freight-only lines.

Chris Austin said: "They are all large towns which have changed radically since the railways went 40 years ago. Many were old coal mining or manufacturing centres, which now generate large numbers of commuters who need to use the train.

"All the schemes, with support from national and local government, could be completed over the next two decades. At the very least the land needs to left as a possible rail corridor, rather than being built on."

Cambridgeshire County Council considered reopening the line between March and Wisbech (not a Beeching

The 19¼ mile Cranleigh line which linked Guildford with Horsham via Cranleigh has been suggested for reopening. The only Surrey casualty of the Beeching Axe, it closed on June 14, 1965 four months before its 100th anniversary. Preserved LSWR T9 4-4-0 No. 120 is seen heading through Baynards station with a special on June 24, 1962. In February 1957 the BBC filmed a version of *The Railway Children* here. The current owners have carefully restored it to its original condition.
MIKE ESAU

Below: **Corby's new state-of-the-art station was opened on February 23, 2009.** When Corby, which lies on the Midland Railway's 'alternative route' between Kettering and Nottingham, closed to passengers in May 1967, the steelworks town with a population of around 40,000 became one of the largest urban areas in Europe without a railway station, although the line remained open for freight. On April 13, 1987 a local council subsidised passenger service was reintroduced with 11 shuttle trains running daily between Corby and Kettering. Despite more than 100,000 people using it within the first 12 months, it became irregular and unreliable, leading to the withdrawal of subsidies, and passenger services were again withdrawn on June 2, 1990. Plans for a second attempt at reopening were approved in 2007 and Corby now has hourly East Midlands Trains services to and from London. ROBIN JONES

History was made on March 11, 2010 when around 8000 people turned out to watch BR Britannia Pacific No. 70013 *Oliver Cromwell* haul the 'Broadsman', first public train over the reinstated level crossing in Station Road, Sheringham, linking Network Rail's Bittern Line from Norwich to the North Norfolk Railway which runs to Holt. Thanks to the volunteer-driven reconnection, Holt now appears for the first time on the electronic destination board at London's Liverpool Street station. ROBIN JONES

closure, but lost its passenger services in 1968) to passengers in 1990. However a quote from British Rail of £1.36 million for the upgrading of the then-operational freight line, combined with a £200,000-a-year operating charge, led to the plan being shelved.

One of the major criticisms made of Beeching was that he failed to take into account future trends like population growth and greater demand for travel.

The ATOC report suggested ways of redressing the balance, although it had to accept that because vacant trackbeds had not been safeguarded, many of those running through urban areas had been built over and would therefore be difficult or impossible to reopen.

The report flew in the face of a White Paper published by the Labour Government in 2007 which said there were no plans to reopen branch lines and even hinted that it might no longer be appropriate to protect their trackbeds from building development.

ATOC suggested that other lines which could be prioritised for reopening include the Uckfield to Lewes line in East Sussex, part of which is now occupied by the Lavender Line, the Bristol to Portishead branch and Yorkshire's Harrogate-Ripon-Northallerton route.

The restoration of the Manton Curve in Rutland would facilitate direct services between Kettering and Peterborough, while reopening the electrified Woodhead

line from Manchester to Sheffield would increase capacity between the two cities.

In 2011, ATOC pointed out that passenger use of existing rural branch lines was very much increasing by as much as 55% in 12 months alone.

It produced figures which showed that passenger levels on the Par to Newquay line rose by 54.8% from 2008/09 to 2009/10, and 56.1% from 2007/08 to 2009/10, while Derby to Matlock rose by 42% and 72.1% and Truro to Falmouth by 37.8% and 56.1%.

It reported that many of the fastest-growing branch lines connect to seaside resorts and towns, and as in the pre-Beeching eras, showed high points during the summer months. Nevertheless, there was an underlying trend of rising passenger numbers on the rural railways, due to the increasing popularity of home-grown attractions, and concerted efforts to attract local people and visitors back to the railways.

Some of the lines saw growth after operators put on more services to meet demand from commuters and holidaymakers alike.

Above: **A Worksop-bound East Midlands Trains Class 158 DMU calls at Mansfield station on the Robin Hood Line, a successful Beeching closure reversal.** ROBIN JONES

Hymek diesel hydraulic D7023 departs from Portishead on August 28, 1964, a week before passenger services were withdrawn. Local people are long campaigning for the rail services to Bristol to be restored, especially in view of the fact that the branch has been reopened for freight traffic as far as nearby Portbury Dock. E T GILL/RM

An undated view of Churston station shows GWR 14XX No. 1470 on a Brixham branch train with a 2-6-2T on a Kingswear service. ATOC has suggested building a park-and-ride for Brixham here, but not the reopening the Brixham branch. GREAT WESTERN SOCIETY

Chapter Fifteen
The final verdict

So what should we really make of Dr Beeching today, almost 60 years after he became British Railways chairman and "the most hated civil servant in Britain".

Was he a bogeyman – or a benefactor?

If we long for the steam era through rose-tinted spectacles, and long for the days when country towns and villages were served by a dense network of cross-country routes and branch lines, which meant that you could travel almost anywhere by train, then he will be damned without redemption by our sentimentality, and we should read no further.

Likewise, if we view the relationship between Transport Minister Ernest Marples, who had vested interests in road building and ended up fleeing Britain with vast unpaid tax bills, and the man he chose to pay a near-popstar salary bring hard-hitting business principles to British Railways at a time when it was plunging ever deeper into a mire of unprecedented debt, we might be forgiven for thinking that dark forces of self interest conspired to bring about the demise of the national network that was, in favour of alternative transport.

Understandably, there was no love lost between Beeching and the tens of thousands of lowly-paid rail workers who

Preserved B1 4-6-0 No. 61264 calls at Stamford in August 2006. Beeching's 1963 report recommended the closure of local stopping services on the Leicester to Peterborough line, and accordingly, in 1966 intermediate village stations such as Ketton & Collyweston and Helpston closed. ROBIN JONES

were left on the scrap heap with meagre pensions by the cutbacks which they considered to be vindictive and impersonal to their dying day, accusing him of mercilessly wielding his axe with vitriol, glee and even spite.

In 1962, there were 474,536 people employed by British Railways – the figure fell to around 307,000 by 1968.

Yet Beeching could not be blamed for their historic low wages and the inherited hopeless level of overstaffing on lines for which public demand was disappearing fast – and maybe their venom might instead have been better directed at former rail passengers who had bought a car.

However, if we place everything in its true context, we must look outside the bubble that is Britain.

The hard fact is that countries throughout the western hemisphere had been closing unremunerative lines since the 1930s. What was happening in Britain in the Fifties and Sixties was also taking place in North America, the continent, where swathes of rural metre gauge lines were being closed, and closer to home, Ireland. Countries like the USA were years ahead of Britain in terms of dieselisation, electrification and route rationalisation.

Everywhere, those in power were also having to come to grips with the unparalled phenomenon of the soaring levels of private motor transport, from motorbikes to luxury cars. It was certainly not a problem limited to Britain, and likewise Beeching and Marples cannot be blamed for the closure trends in other countries. Indeed, global evidence indicates that closures at this time were unavoidable.

Dr Richard Beeching was awarded a controversial salary typical of the higher-paid private sector than a civil servant. He was also given a remit, which broadly said that the deficit must be cut at all costs, and he was given scant leeway to recommend that loss-making lines should be retained on social grounds. Such judgment was ultimately left to Marples, who did redeem some routes recommended for the axe by Beeching, and who has also been accused of delaying other closures as the 1964 general election loomed.

The hard fact is that some railway lines running in the Fifties and Sixties should never have been built at all, because they had been designed and built more than a century ago in starkly different socio-economic conditions, with hope of riches that never materialised.

Other lines had become so poorly patronised that it would have been cheaper to pay for the daily users to share a taxi.

Take the GWR's Cheltenham to Kingham and Banbury route, for instance. How many people would travel daily to Cheltenham or Banbury from, say, Bourton-on-the-Water or Chipping Norton? Take away the line's coal and agricultural traffic, and what business case do you have left?

One often-expounded argument against Beeching was the failure to recognise the full importance of loss leaders. Closing any branch line eradicated its traffic contribution to the main line. In fact, this aspect was addressed in The Reshaping of British Railways, although his response was not as flexible as it might have been.

Beeching and others assumed that disenfranchised villagers would merely use motor transport to reach the nearest main line station, and so often they were proved wrong.

On the other hand, by the early Sixties many remote branch lines had so few regular passengers that their revenue contribution to the main line was negligible, and in these cases, it is difficult to argue with Beeching.

The savings that Beeching promised to make never materialised. By closing almost a third of the network, he managed to achieve a saving of just £30 million, while overall losses were still above £100 million.

His 'Mark 2' report in 1965 which caused for even more drastic closures, disenfranchising large regions as well as

Below: **A typical but rarely-photographed post-Beeching scene: the goods yard at Alston being demolished after the withdrawal of goods services in September 1966. The passenger platform is still intact beyond the Drott bulldozer working in the ruins of the goods shed. The Alston-Haltwhistle passenger service escaped the immediate axe and lasted until May 3, 1976 due to poor road connections in the area. Alston is now the terminus of the 2ft gauge South Tynedale Railway.**
ALAN EARNSHAW

John Sergeant's view of Beeching

In spring 2011, veteran television reporter John Sergeant used Scotland's Bo'ness & Kinneil Railway as a backdrop to an item on the Beeching Cuts he recorded for BBC's *The One Show*.

A special train hauled by Class 26 diesel No. 26024 did two trips from Bo'ness to Birkhill to allow the film crew to get "the train in motion effect" while John did an interview.

Travelling with John was rail expert David Spaven who provided detailed examples of how the cuts savaged the UK network by about a third.

John said: "We think of Beeching as being a bad guy. We think, looking back, if we hadn't had this guy, lots of lovely railways could have been preserved.

"But it was very much a problem of the time and people thought that railways then were old fashioned and they were uneconomic. So something had to be done – and that was a savage reappraisal of the entire railway network.

"My conclusion is that Beeching is neither a hero nor a villain but very much a man of his time."

John Sergeant is pictured with his crew: Rick Goodwin, producer, left, Jamie Gavin, runner and soundman, and cameraman Gordon Ross.

---

towns and village from the network, was such an embarrassment that he parted company with British Railways soon after, and ahead of schedule.

Yet if the rationale behind the 1963 report was so wrong, why did Harold Wilson's Labour Government which had publicly pledged to stop the Beeching cuts before winning the general election in 1964 not only immediately renege on its promises, but in some cases speeded up the closures.

Labour Transport Minister Barbara Castle introduced a key social element which led to the potential retention of unviable lines, and set in place the Passenger Transport Executive model by which integrated urban transport could be – as happened successfully – developed, but let us not forget she still closed thousands of miles of routes as recommended by Beeching and then added several more routes into the bargain. A strong element of the recognition of the fact that widespread closures in a car-dominated country inevitable appears here.

In a great decade of change, when the steam era that had served the country so well during two world wars was visibly disappearing, with new futuristic forms of transport jumping off the drawing board, and where the car provided a liberating force to even modest income families, there were those who believed that modernised or not, the days of the railways were numbered.

The biggest failing of all

For me, the biggest mistake of the Beeching era and the years that followed was the speed and ruthlessness by which closures were implemented, leaving little possibility of going back should circumstances change – as they have done.

New towns were appearing on the landscape, and with inner-city redevelopment, sizeable communities were springing up on the outskirts of cities. Meanwhile, country towns and villages that previously could not support their local branch line would eventually add housing estates and become much-sought-after commuter belt settlements.

With soaring levels of car ownership, surely it was obvious that rush-hour gridlock in cities would occur within the foreseeable future, and buses without dedicated lanes would fare no better than cars in jams. Where there are bus lanes, they so often serve the purpose of slowing cars to snail's pace in the remaining lane – often people need their car for their job, and using public transport is not an option.

Countries like France got it right. Yes, withdraw the worst loss-making services, but keep the trackbed, if not the track itself, intact for potential future use should circumstances change.

In Britain, such options were discarded too quickly or never even considered, tracks being lifted sometimes within days of closure leaving no going back, and the land sold off.

The problem is that any land that is sold off in urban areas will be sooner rather than later redeveloped. The cost of repurchasing former railway land in cities and demolishing buildings in the way of any reinstatement schemes immediately makes most of them non-viable. Building new termini on the edges of urban areas rather than in their centres defeats the object.

What had long rankled with me is the case of the closure of the GWR Stratford-upon-Avon to Cheltenham line, which in post-Beeching years had been retained for freight. In 1976, more than a decade after Beeching, a derailment at Chicken Curve near Winchcombe damaged the track and led to a British Rail decision not to bother repairing the line. Most of the 28 mile route was lifted three years later, and the trackbed through Stratford used for a town bypass, although a grass strip capable of accommodating a single track was left.

Fast forward a third of a century, and the houses now built around the site in Stratford have changed hands many times. While in the late Nineties, Network Rail's predecessor Railtrack was seriously looking at reopening the route for freight as a bypass for the Lickey Incline, I have no doubt that there would now be an overwhelming 'not in my back yard' protest, as well as problems with crossing the new roadway on the level.

Had the trackbed been preserved intact, while letting everyone know that the railway might come back one day, this situation and many others like it would be avoided.

I once looked at badly-gridlocked Bath, and attempts being made to regenerate the former coalmining towns of Radstock and Midsomer Norton. Why not, I wondered, reinstate the Somerset & Dorset main line linking all three, as a commuter route, so people could buy cheap housing and commute to Bath and Bristol? I was informed as a rough estimate that it would cost at least as much in actual pounds (forgetting inflation) to rebuild that section of line as Beeching managed to save by closing an entire third of Britain's rail network.

What if?

What if Dr Richard Beeching had never been appointed in 1961?

The regions of British Railways would certainly have closed more and more branch lines as they had been doing for several years, probably without any reference to a central guiding criteria.

Allowing them to carry on doing their own thing may have ended up with the network's finances in an even greater mess, and maybe lead to more closures than were recommended by the Beeching report.

It is worth pausing for a minute, looking back on the maps in this volume, and then seriously asking – how many of the Beeching closures would have happened in the sixties anyway, with or without him?

Similarly, another person in Beeching's place might well have closed more lines sooner, before the subsequent and enlightened social need policies of later years could save them.

Furthermore, if the recommended cutbacks had not been made at the time, and the British Railways deficit left to spiral further out of control, with only vain hopes being thrown at it, would the delay have ultimately led to far more drastic rationalisation being imposed, such as that outlined in the horror story that was the Serpell report in 1982, and with the full blessing of the over-burdened taxpayer? We will never know.

Nothing anyone could have done would have prevented the rise of the car and the mass exodus of passengers from rail to road, which offers greater personal flexibility. It was a global phenomenon, not unique to Britain.

What was being attempted by Beeching, however, was the identification of instances where passengers would still prefer to travel by train, as well as cases where the carriage of freight by rail offered clear advantages over road haulage. While there may have been elements of tunnel vision in both the remit he was given by Ernest Marples and his approach, he made an honest attempt to achieve these goals and thereby save the railway network from a far more dire predicament.

Oh Doctor Beeching! was a TV sitcom written by David Croft and Richard Spendlove, which ran for two series in the mid-Nineties. It was set at the small fictional branch line railway station of Hatly, which is threatened with closure under the Beeching Axe. The programme was filmed at Arley station on the Severn Valley Railway.

He applied a simple business principle.

A factory employs 20 men on the production line. Suddenly someone invents machinery that can do the job of 19 of them, leaving just one to oversee it. That one position is what may then be termed a 'real' job – it is essential for production to be maintained and cannot be replaced by technology, and the other 19 should therefore be made redundant, according to the accountant's recommendation.

The accountant's remit by nature is ruthless and cannot involve consideration as to whether sacking the 19 would cause hardship, or the loss of their incomes would have a negative effect on the local economy outside and so on. That final decision is up to the factory owners.

In the case of British Railways, Beeching was the accountant, and the owners were the Conservative and Labour Governments. The buck stopped with them.

However, if the powers that be outside the firm look at the redundancies in a wider context, such as the cost of

Below left: GWR prairie tank No. 5541 heads a train at Tavistock South on June 16, 1962. The last passenger trains from Launceston to Plymouth via Tavistock were scheduled to run on December 29, 1962, the closure to passengers taking effect from the following Monday, December 31. However, heavy snowfalls quashed any bid to commemorate the end of the GWR branch. The 6.20am Plymouth terminated at Tavistock at 12.20am the following day, while the 7.10am Tavistock to Plymouth was stranded at Bickleigh overnight, nature holding off the end for another day. Beeching had a point here, because this route largely mirrored the Southern Railway main line from Plymouth to Exeter, but that also closed, in 1968. In 2011, talks were underway about rebuilding the latter route south to Bere Alston, re-enfranchising a town with more than 11,000 inhabitants.
GREAT WESTERN TRUST

Beeching: 55 Years of the Axe Man 129

unemployment benefit, retraining, supporting local business deprived of income from the workers who have lost their wage, and so on, they might well decide that a subsidy to the factory to retain some of the jobs, maybe in the event of increased production at a later date, would serve the local economy well.

No country has been able to support a large railway network of its original size and a modern road network side by side.

Economies were inevitable, but who knows what lines might have been saved if the social aspect of closures had been more fully addressed by transport ministers some years before Barbara Castle's 1968 Act, maybe even as soon as the pledge-breaking Harold Wilson came to power in 1964?

For a man accused of trying to destroy Britain's railways, Beeching's innovations regarding bulk freight such as the Merry-Go-Round coal hoppers and the Freightliner container system proved highly successful and are still in use nearly half a century on.

So much changed in the Sixties, including the nationalised railway network, which emerged from the decade streamlined and slimmed down, even if it was never as sleek and shiny as those who told us that the Seventies were 'The Age of the Train' in TV advertising would have had us believe.

Yes, rationalisation could and almost certainly should have been done better, and while the Sixties promised so much hope and optimism, the decade came packaged with liberal lashings of naiveté and lack of real foresight in so many cases.

Nonetheless, the reduced railway network has managed to ride the storm of threats to its existence like the Serpell report, and with the opening of the High Speed 1 Channel Tunnel rail link to the award-winning St Pancras International station, and the promise of a new high-speed rail link from London to Birmingham, Manchester and the north, and an east-to-west cross-link line beneath London, and passenger figures at their highest in many decades, the future for rail is now looking more promising than at any time since the 1955 Modernisation Plan.

We all miss the rural branch lines, look at them wistfully in magazines like *Heritage Railway* and on archive cine

Closures of loss-making line were going full steam ahead on throughout the UK in the Fifties and Sixties – and Dr Beeching had no control over any of them. Waiting to leave the terminus of the doomed Warrenpoint branch in Ulster with a return Sunday outing to Belfast on August 30, 1964 was Class S 4-4-0 No. 48. RW COLE/RM

footage, and we know that the closure of trunk routes like the Great Central was short sighted. Too many large towns became cut off from the network, and not enough emphasis was placed on the fear that motor transport would at the rate of expansion bring cities to gridlock sooner than later.

Yet evidence, backed by a mountain of hindsight, shows that while Beeching made mistakes, he appeared to honestly and efficiently follow a given remit, albeit one that was too brutal in parts.

The cutbacks, while largely inevitable, may also be viewed as having reshaped Britain's railways into a slimmer, fitter beast that at last, after disappointing decades in the doldrums, is now gearing up to the fresh challenges of the 21st century, able to hold its head high in an age where the car will forever remain king.

Yes, it is so easy to make Dr Beeching a scapegoat, especially when you take into account the speed and clinical efficiency in which he went about his deficit-cutting task. He merely took the queen's shilling and carried out the duties he was given by not one but two democratically-elected Governments, on both sides of the political fence.

In trying to make sense of global transport trends at the beginning of the greatest decade of change, the like of which had never been seen before, he steadfastly and determinedly tackled a job which under no circumstances was ever likely to bring him universal popularity, and led to him taking the public rap for the final decisions of those in higher authority on both sides of the political fence, both during and after his term in office.

Maybe this particular hatchet man erred more of the side of the heroic than any of us want to believe.

Baron Beeching lived in Lewes Road, East Grinstead, from the 1960s until he died at Queen Victoria Hospital in 1985. Beeching Way in East Grinstead was named after him as it lies on the route of one of the lines made obsolete by his report.

He first developed signs of heart trouble in 1969. The following year, he became chairman of building materials group Redland plc, and later became chairman of ship owners Furness Withy.

When once asked about his career with the railways, and if he regretted his cuts, he famously and somewhat pompously said that he regretted not having closed more lines. He maintained this stance to the end.

The Bluebell Railway, where as we saw in Chapter 3, he opened a new halt in 1962, months before the publication of The Reshaping of British Railways, at time of writing this publication in 2011 was steaming ahead with plans to complete its northern extension to rejoin the main line at East Grinstead. That project is now complete.

Irony abounds from many angles.

BEECHING WAY

More information

*Anyone wishing to know more about Dr Beeching should make the National Railway Museum's Search Engine facility their first port of call.

Search Engine, the York Museum's library and archive centre, is open every day except December 24-26, seven days a week, from 10am to 5.30pm, and offers unparalleled research facilities to the general public.

You can browse railway books and magazines, listen to oral history recordings from people working on the railways, watch railway films and DVDs, access original materials including documents and artefacts, access WiFi and find a quiet area to study.

For further details visit http://www.nrm.org.uk or email search.engine@nrm.org.uk

Another great resource is the Railway Magazine's fully-searchable digital archive – www.railwaymagazine.co.uk